From Party Line to Mobile Phone

Extraordinary Unassuming Determined
Philanthropist and Professional Volunteer

Kate B. Webster

Sunt Press

For information
Kate B. Webster Estate
kdk@kdkragen.com

Compiled and Edited by:
    K. D. Kragen
    KaveDragen Ink LLC
    kavedragenink.com

Book design by Sarah E. Holroyd (https://sleepingcatbooks.com)
Book Shepherd Trudy B. Catterfeld, BookMarketingNext
Front cover and back cover design by Anita Jones, Anotherjonesgraphics
Front and back cover image work Jim Dittmer, JDA Creative Color
Interior image work Nick Felkey, Exceptional Images
Peter B. Webster back cover drawing of Seattle, WA, front book matter drawing of New York
    and Seattle

Published 2019

ISBN-13: 978-1-7330320-0-1

Library of Congress Control Number: 2019905721

Sunt Press, Bainbridge Island, Washington

The Great Oak, Lo-An-Oak, Far Hills, New Jersey (Artwork by M. Conklin). Used with permission

Artist Peter B. Webster bridges Kate B. Webster's life's journey from New York to Seattle.

Dedication

To my children, grandchildren and "greats" who continue with love to support my determination to explore and experience as much of our world as possible

Lo-An-Oak – The Great Oak Tree, Far Hills, New Jersey

The Big House, Lo-An-Oak, Far Hills, New Jersey

Contents

Author's Introduction — 1

Part I — 3
New York Stories — 5
Sunnybranch, Lo-An-Oak, Far Hills, New Jersey — 31
Smith College — 45

Part II — 57
Washington Stories — 59
Julia Child Comes To Dinner — 80
Family Picture Album — 83
Kelly's And Annie's Weddings — 87

Part III — 91
The Professional Volunteer — 93
The Maytime Ball — 98
My Years At Children's Hospital — 100
Washington State University — 104
Smith College Board — 107
The Bishop Foundation — 110
The Island School — 112
Grace Church — 114
Kate B. Webster Medical Pavilion Children's Hospital — 116
Lessons Of Being A Professional Volunteer — 117

Part IV — 121
Anne Mae Seligman Belcher — 123
The Seligman Story — 127
Harold Stewart Belcher — 132
The 2000 Belcher Family Reunion — 134

Part V — 139
The Story of Pacific Air Freight & Airborne Express — 141
Recollections Of Holt — 159

Part VI — 167
Holt Wilson Webster & Craig Lewis Webster — 169

Part VII — 191
Travels With Kate — 193

Addendum — 215
Kate's Dogs — 217
Kate Belcher Webster, Accomplishments — 221
References & Sources — 223
Acknowledgements — 224

Author's Introduction

Memories, memories. What a wonderful word. There is a rhythm in its sound that is comforting, a plurality which is inclusive and warm.

Why does anyone feel compelled to share recollections of a life which, though happy and full and highly satisfactory, is not extraordinary? It could be classified as the story of just another pebble on the shores of humanity. But, upon reflection, after more than eight decades of life, the vast changes on so many levels and especially the difference in opportunities for women that continue to evolve, have led me to tell my story, much of which can now be called "stories from a great grandmother."

My life has spanned three-fourths of the twentieth century and over a decade into the twenty-first. So many changes that most people only read about have been an everyday part of my life. These myriad experiences have contributed to my expectation of change, to my curiosity about what will happen next, what new wonders will be discovered and how these events will impact the world and affect our own lives. These experiences have also challenged me to try to learn and accept new ideas and lifestyles.

Perhaps I will be the only reader of my recollections. But I am enjoying the trip back—and quite honestly want to get it down before the pictures fade and the recollections become dim.

While these memories are in chronological order, throughout this epistle one may stumble upon an occasional non-sequitur vignette. These unexpected episodes have provided delightful moments for me and have contributed to my understanding of the world around us.

Nana With Her Kate (c. 1926)

Part I

New York Stories

The Laundry Basket

Hannah, our housekeeper, said "Come with me."

We walked down the hall, a very dark hall, of our first apartment. She took my hand as we entered the dining room, which was the only room in the house that ever had any sun in it.

Sunshine filled the room, and I noticed a laundry basket near the window. Walking slowly over to the basket – background music to our life then was always the Third Avenue Elevated, what we called "The El" – Hannah said, "Go look in the laundry basket."

I peeked down into it, and there was a little baby! It was my sister, Suzie. I didn't really know she was coming. But there she was! She looked like a doll, and I thought I could pick her up.

Hannah said, "No, dear. You'll have to wait awhile."

But it wasn't too long before she was old enough to play with.

We lived in New York City on East 46th Street, between Third Avenue and Lexington, on the south side of the street. It was one of those old brownstone houses that had been converted into apartments. In the center of the block, everybody had a little backyard garden, so there was a lot of sun shining on the back of the houses.

Hannah Morris, was an Irish lady with gray hair piled on top of her head. She had a lovely brogue and a warm personality and also was a

Baby Kate, Dad & Cousins

5

great cook and kept a tidy house. Hannah stayed with us from the time I was born until I was ten years old.

This very first memory of my new sister goes back to late summer 1926 when I was almost two and a half years old.

Uncle John Squibb

(Distantly Related To The Squibb Pharmaceutical Family[1])

My other memories of that early life, on 46th Street, are scattered. There were two bedrooms, a bath, a dining room, a kitchen. There was a fire escape ladder going down to the garden. The Third Avenue "EL"[2] clattered by steadily, and it became a constant background to our lives there—white noise. We got so we never paid any attention to it.

Mother and Dad, both practicing physicians, went to work every day, but they spent all their spare time with Suzie and me. They started reading to us when we were very young.

The living room was in the front of the house, right on 46th Street. It wasn't very big, but it was where we all gathered. We could see the people walking by.

1   The two Squibb images courtesy Bristol-Myers Squibb: http://www.bms.com/ourcompany/Pages/history.aspx
2   Image: "A train passes Cooper Square in the 1950s, with the Empire State Building in the background. Image source: https://commons.wikimedia.org/wiki/File:Third_Ave_El_-_1.jpg

For several years there, Uncle John Squibb was a member of our family. He suffered from rheumatoid arthritis, walked with crutches, and worked in Uncle Charlie Ashmun's travel office, Charles Ashmun, Inc., on Fifth Avenue.

Uncle John's family lived in New Jersey, and it was difficult for him to commute, that's why he stayed with us in those years. Part of the living-room had been curtained-off with heavy velvet curtains so he could have some privacy. Uncle John was a delightful man with all kinds of stories. My sister and I loved to sit and listen to him while Mom and Dad were out.

The New York Subway

It was while living in that apartment that my father took me on my first subway ride. The subway entrance was on 42nd Street and Lexington Avenue, so it wasn't very far away. That's the way Dad went to work every morning, down to the lower part of the city, near Wall Street.

At first I was very frightened, going down the long stairs below ground, hearing the noisy trains come and go. But Dad was very calm. We stood waiting hand in hand on the platform, got on the train, and then it was pretty exciting!

I don't recall much else about those days. Every weekend, in the spring and the fall, from Easter through Thanksgiving, we would go out to grandmother Kate Belcher's house in Far Hills, New Jersey and spend the weekend. In the winter time, when Nana (grandmother) moved back from Far Hills to Newark, we would often go there on the weekends.

That is about the limit of my recollections of life at 46th Street.

Gramercy Park

When I was almost four, we moved to 34 East Gramercy Park on East 20th Street. The apartment house is still there, right across from the park. We moved at first into an apartment on the top, 8th floor.

Soon after, my sister Suzie developed a terrible case of TB.

We had a French governess named Anna, and Hannah was still the housekeeper. Anna came from the city of Brest, in Brittany, France. A lovely, ruddy-faced young woman, curly dark hair. She was probably in her early 20s, if she was that old. We both loved her.

She apparently arrived in America with the TB virus, which nobody realized. My sister, being one and a half or two years old, was carried around a lot by Anna, and before long Suzie developed TB.

She was very sick. The doctors told Mother and Dad that she really should go to Switzerland, but they didn't think she was strong enough to stand the boat trip. In her own inimitable fashion, Mother said, "She is not going to die. We will save her."

Although it never occurred to me that my sister might die, that remark was typical of my mother's determination and confidence in her own ability to make things happen.

One of the difficult measures they had to take was to do a bronchoscopy. That procedure entails going down into the lungs and pulling out a big plug of mucus; and in those days there was no anesthetic for infants. My father told me about it many years later and said it was the worst thing he had ever had to watch. (Before the 1970s, a bronchoscopy was done with a rigid bronchoscope, generally under anesthesia, but again, not for infants.) When they pulled out the bronchoscope, and she could breathe again, she said, "All done, all done, all done!" This became one of her favorite phrases in her childhood.

Suzie did survive, just as our mother had predicted.

Accompanied by either Mother or Hannah, Suzie and I spent that entire winter and spring of 1929 up on the roof of 34 Gramercy Park, because it was healthy! We stayed up there on sunny days and many gray days, too, if anybody can believe that today—but it was the 1920s and the air was clean on the roof of our eight-story apartment house. Mother and Dad couldn't afford to go to Switzerland or do anything else to help Suzie recuperate.

From the photos taken there, one can tell Suzie seemed to have enjoyed it!

Being incarcerated in her crib, Suzie didn't move around very much. She sat there or napped most of the time. Hannah had her book and her chair, and she would be there for us and tell us stories. I had dolls that I loved to play with and some books to look at. It was an easy and relaxed time; it was just what we did that year.

Sister Suzie (Mother on the left) up on the roof of Gramercy Park apartment, 1928.

I turned five. While Suzie continued to get better she was still frail.

Between Christmas and spring vacation Mother and Dad sent me to stay with Aunt Mary and Uncle Charlie Ashmun in Newark, New Jersey. The Ashmuns lived in a beautiful house, at 400 Clifton Avenue. It was a warm and cozy place, especially out on Aunt Mary's sun room where it seemed always bright and cheerful. Canaries singing, the scent of flowered pots, it was a happy place to play.

At that time, my cousins Charlie "Chil" Ashmun, George "Geo," and Johnny lived in the house. I had the guestroom. The house was just across the road from Mt. Pleasant Elementary. Johnny, who was a year older than I, attended kindergarten. Once in a while, I was allowed to go with him and spend the day. It was a treat and made me feel "grown-up"!

Sophie, their German governess, was a wonderfully warm person. Occasionally she made a graham cracker cake with white icing. It was amazing. (I've tried for years to copy this creation or to discover the recipe. I think I'm pretty close to it now, it has taken that long.)

The boys had a locomotive set in their playroom on the third floor, and I learned all the parts of a train and how to put the tracks together. All in all, it was a time when I felt loved and cared for.

Aunt Mary was my God-mother, and although I never had any brothers, from my ear-

Gramercy Park bronze sculpture of Edwin Thomas Booth, famous local actor, produced in 1917 by Edmund Thomas Quinn (1868-1929).

liest recollection the Ashmun boys treated me like a little sister, and I loved them all.

While Suzie's health continued to improve, it took her more than a couple of years to fully recover. As she gained strength, we would go across the street to Gramercy Park, where we spent the afternoons or part of every day.

Gramercy Park is much the same today as it was back then. It took up a

The Convalescent 1928

Winter 1927-1928

Dad, Kate, Johnny & Sid Dillon, Winter 1927-1928

Kate & Suzie 1929

whole city block. In 1831 developer Samuel B. Ruggles bought Gramercy Farm from James Duane to establish a private open space for the surrounding community; in 1833 an eight foot wrought iron fence, with spikes on the top, ran all the way around it. There were four locked gates, one on each side. It had—and still does have—gravel paths, and lawns which no one was allowed to walk on. As a child I learned to play hop-scotch and jump-rope and ride a bike on gravel! My knees

Kate & Johnny, Comrades

(probably that's what's wrong with them today) never recovered. They were scabbed all the time.

As we got older, Hannah wouldn't go to Gramercy Park with us anymore. We would be locked in the park after school by our apartment doorman, and he would tell us what time he would come and get us. There was a big Prudential Insurance Company clock tower that we could see from the middle of the park and know what time it was.

It sounds a little like jail today, but there were lots of kids our age there, from all over the area! We just enjoyed playing together. There were no bathrooms in the park. It was a very different world, but we had good times together, and amazingly there were never any fights!

When it came time for me to go to kindergarten, Mother decided that it would be better for Suzie if I stayed home one more year to keep her company as she continued to recover and regain her strength. To this day, my only regret at missing kindergarten was that I never learned to cut-and-paste.

Suzie went to kindergarten two years later. Mother was called after the second week to discuss Suzie's problem, namely that she was just sitting in the corner, not entering into any activities. When Mother questioned Suzie, she replied, "I didn't come to school to play; I want to learn." This didn't surprise Mom, and she encouraged the teacher to put her daughter to work.

Far Hills Sandbox, 1928

Me and my sister Suzie, Lo-An-Oak, 1929-30

Friends Seminary

The next fall was my first year of school at the Friends Seminary, E. 16th St. and Rutherford Place, near Stuyvesant Square, just south of Gramercy Park. A Quaker school serving kindergarten through 12th grade, Friends was founded in 1786—and is, to this day, New York City's oldest continuing co-educational school.

My first school experience, therefore, started with first grade. My teacher was Mrs. Rice. A fairly short, trim lady, Mrs. Rice was very chatty yet nonetheless businesslike. Actually, she reminded me a bit of Mother. She was strict, but she was also warm.

The best part of first grade, and perhaps my most vivid memory, was learning to read. We had Dick And Jane or something similar for our first readers. At home, my father read to us constantly; he encouraged me to read by myself, and we would also go through books together.

Friends Seminary offered a wonderful introduction to education for me, and, I suspect, to most children. It was warm. It was caring and friendly. Some of the teachers were Quakers, and they were committed to a learning approach which taught kids to really enjoy what they were doing and to not be afraid of trying anything.

My second grade teacher's name was Miss Hawk. She was a big woman, large-boned and tall; I thought she was well-named, because she had a big nose that reminded me of a hawk—which probably was totally unfair.

Early in the year each of us was told that we would have to give a five-minute talk to the whole class, sometime during the winter semester, on any topic we chose.

For some reason—and to this day I will never understand why—I decided I would give a talk about spiders. I don't like spiders. I never liked spiders. They scared me. My father introduced me to an encyclopedia, and he guided me through the process of finding out about what I needed to know. I ended up deciding to talk about the black widow spider; she sounded exciting!

When it came my turn to present this first speech of my life, I was terrified! However, somehow I got carried away, and Miss Hawk had to stop me. (I've given many, many speeches in my life, but that was the first, and it was one I will never forget.)

My third grade teacher was Mrs. Stuart. My only recollection of third grade was that in the Christmas play I was Mrs. Santa Claus. I was chubby in those days. I didn't like being chubby, but Santa Claus was chubby too, and we did have a good time.

Miss Kelsey taught fourth grade. We studied English history, and I learned about King Arthur. I still have the original book of stories about King Arthur which I received in fourth grade. I loved it all. I had turned into an avid reader at that point.

Fifth grade was Mrs. Mercer, and it was there I had my first introduction to American history. She was a wonderful history teacher, full of stories, but always stressed the theme of how we started and why we started as a nation, and our relationship to England. She also talked of our mistreatment of the Indian tribes.

In sixth grade, my last year at Friends Seminary, my teacher was Miss Semens. Sixth grade was a ball! I found out I was very good at math, and I enjoyed the beginning of algebra that year.

That was also the year I went to my first dance. There were only four girls in sixth grade and twelve boys. One of them became my first date and dance partner. His name was Dick Hunter. We still correspond every once-in-awhile. His father, Earle Hunter, was vice-president of the school. Mr. Hunter was a formidable-looking and somewhat "scary" man; to me, he looked like Abraham Lincoln.

I went to my first dance at the school with Dick. A week later we had our first date when he invited me to have lunch at his house. I had a hard time trying to figure out—as females do forever—what to wear. It was a Saturday morning, and I finally picked out a blue-print cotton dress. My mother said I should wear long, knee-length stockings with it, but I wanted to wear bobby socks, which had just come into fashion. We had a big fight. She won. At least the stockings were blue and went with the dress.

One teacher at Friends whom I was especially impressed with was Miss Brooks, the art teacher. A real Quaker, it was always "thee" and "thou." She was a tall woman with braids around her head neatly done up every morning. I was not good at drawing, but Miss Brooks showed me such patience, she was always such an encouragement to me.

The only thing I could ever draw (even to this day) was a square house with a tree, a child on a swing, smoke coming out of the chimney—I was very proud that it looked like smoke—and steps going up to the front door of the house. Mrs. Brooks would say to me, "Well, that's very good, Kate. Do you think you could add any people?" "No. I don't think so. I don't know how to draw people"—except for the little girl swinging on the swing, which was pretty much a stick-figure. She was so patient with me, and understanding. All she said was "Just keep trying."

Interestingly, when I got to Brearley, we had to take art from Miss Carpenter, who was not my favorite teacher at all. She would say, "Kate, you are not trying! You've got to learn to draw." And I would answer, "I can't. It's just not in me." Mrs. Carpenter was very impatient with me. The difference between the two teachers made a big impression. (Happily, I have three children who are all artistic and creative in different ways, two of them extremely talented in drawing! It all comes from the Webster side of the family, not mine.)

An aside: Even though I'd switched from Friends Seminary to Brearley after sixth grade, I went back to visit Friends Seminary in 1991 for my 50th reunion. I was in New York at the time and decided to attend their reunion. It was really just a lunch for the old-timers. We made our own nametags, so I wrote Kate Webster, then thought, nobody's going to know who Kate Webster is, so I changed it to Kate Belcher Webster. A minute later, I felt a tap on my back and it was Dick! He said, "Hi, Kate." Amazing! We did recognize each other. He's been happily married. An engineer. And he had retained his sense of humor.

Our Two Doctors

During our Friends Seminary and Gramercy Park years, there was another dimension in the lives of the Belcher girls, as many of our family friends used to call sister Suzie and me. One of the great gifts we were given during those formative years was the role of our father, Dr. Harold Belcher. The relationship shared by Mother—we mostly called her Mom—and Dad was an unusual one for its time, and, I believe, rarely observed even today. They were both physicians. Mom was an ear, nose, and throat specialist, called an otolaryngologist, or an ENT doctor. Dad was a general practitioner, known at that time as a family doctor.

On Thursday evenings, throughout the 1930s and 40s, one night a week Mother and Dad would spend the evening with friends—separately. Mother attended a weekly bridge game with three medical colleagues. Dad, with his violin, participated in a musical quartette, a classical jam session.

Dad & Mother, c. 1925

Mom had a strong internal drive to excel, and building and maintaining her practice was always her first priority. Dad and Mom started out sharing an office. After six months they real-

ized that in order to stay happily married, they would need to separate during the working day. Mother kept their office at 20 East 53rd Street, while Dad moved down to Wall Street to become "the physician to the Stock Exchange."

Dad kept that job right through the Depression years and World War II. At the end of the war the economy got back to normal, and there was no more need for a physician's office at the Stock Exchange. At that point, Dad set up his own practice on Wall Street, and Mother kept working out of the 53rd Street office. She worked there for 65 years. She actually did move once, from the 8th floor to the 3rd floor. She never modernized her office much, though she did upgrade her equipment occasionally. Her patients always teased about her outdated magazines!

The world of technology never entered Mother's life. In fact, one of the reasons she finally retired was that the state of New York declared they would no longer pay for Medicare patients unless their records were on computers—Mother refused to comply, all her records remaining on index cards. During all her years of medical practice, she worked five and a half days a week, Saturday's until two PM.

After WWII, Mother decided to stop having patients call for appointments. She knew that often one "might wake up with a bad sinus or cough and need to be taken care of as soon as possible." While Mom was basically pragmatic, she was not a creative person; however, she did create a new way to schedule her patients. She put a legal yellow pad on the waiting room table, and people signed in as they arrived and

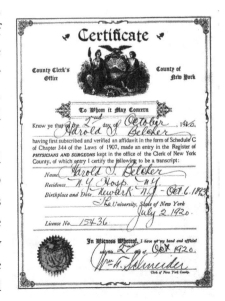

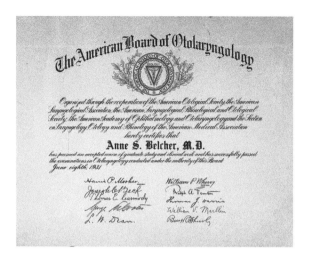

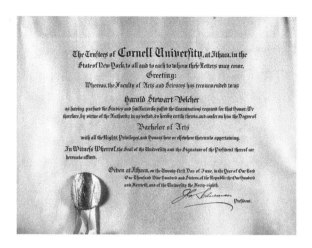

were taken to see Dr. Anne in the order of arrival. The only exception she ever made was for Jackie Kennedy. "Mrs. K" always walked back to the private office and was cared for promptly. Mom's patients were grateful to be able to be taken care of the day they needed her skills.

In August of 1959, Mom and Dad's annual visit to Holt and me on Bainbridge Island was interrupted by a phone call from then Senator John Kennedy's secretary. "The senator has lost his voice," the secretary said, explaining Kennedy was to debate Senator Humphrey in the presidential nomination debates. Mother said, "I can't make it. We're on the West Coast and can't get a flight." A half hour later, the secretary called back. "We've got a 1st class seat for you for

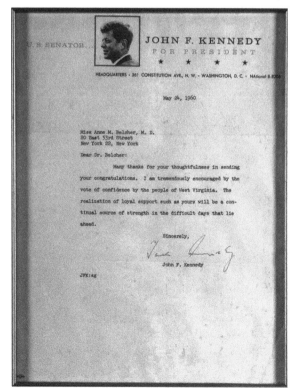

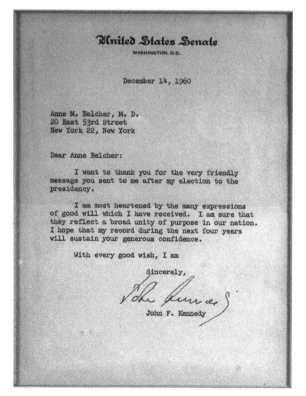

tomorrow morning. We'll get you back to Bainbridge Island in 24 hours. Mother went. Kennedy got his voice back. The rest was history.

In early 1963 Mother was called by Dr. Janet Travell, then President John F. Kennedy's back specialist, to give the president a treatment and have a visit with her friend JBK, Jacqueline Bouvier Kennedy.

Dr. Anne Belcher with Jackie Kennedy & Maurice Tempelsman at her retirement party, June 1992.

January 18, 1963

THE WHITE HOUSE
WASHINGTON

let me know when she gets here   JBK

Dr. Anne Belcher will take the 8 a.m. flight from New York on Wednesday, January 23, and will be available to see you at your convenience that morning

Janet Travell

Dad put in a more typical five day work week, and so it was that Saturdays became Dad's day with his daughters. Each weekend he would take us on an excursion in or close to the City. Sometimes we would visit the Aquarium. (It is long gone now but used to be way down on Lower Manhattan looking out at the Statue Of Liberty.) We would wander through the Wall Street area, including the famous Trinity Church and cemetery.

All the while, Dad would tell us stories about the early days of New York City, its people, and its history. We visited most of the City's museums, including Dad's favorite, the Museum Of Natural History on Central Park West, with skeletons of dinosaurs, whales and other large animals, and the famous Hall Of African Animals (all stuffed), which was started by Teddy Roosevelt. The New York Planetarium was also housed there. Dad especially loved astronomy. (Because of these

Newark Academy ~ Graduating class of 1912
HSB top row, second from right

excursions, especially to the planetarium, I have never lost my interest in astronomy.) Dad had seen Haley's Comet on April 20th, 1910, and he was thrilled to see it again on February 9th, 1986, just two years before he passed away. (For you younger readers, Haley's Comet is due again some-time in July of 2061. It's a family tradition; somebody should be there to mark its famous passing.)

Dad was a creature of habit. He could be flexible when required but preferred to follow his own schedule whenever possible. One of his favorite routines was his daily lunch during the many years he worked as "the physician" to the Stock Exchange. He would go down to the drug store at the basement of the Exchange, sit at the lunch counter and order a liverwurst sandwich and a mug of tomato soup. Actually, he never had to "order" because a few moments after sitting down the treats would be placed before him. The menu never changed, and Dad really enjoyed the predictability of that half-hour in the basement.

During these years, weekends would find all of us together. On Saturday, Mother and Dad would take the "Tube" under the East River to Newark, New Jersey, have dinner with Dad's parents, and then return home.

The next day, Sunday, would always just be the four of us.

I never realized—until I was married, and had children—how Mom and Dad really had decided that medical practice, raising children, and a social life were just too much, too difficult to coordinate. Years later, Mom told me that she and Dad had, early on, made a conscious deci-sion that their social life was on hold until the children were grown. They did entertain couples, or small groups, and Suzie and I were always allowed to have dinner with them. They were most often all physicians or professional acquaintances, and the conversation was always medical, so Suzie and I didn't stay around too long after dinner.

Looking back on it now, it seems like an unusual act of selflessness on the part of Mom and Dad.

My sophomore year at college, when Suzie and I were both away, I called Mother one day to say I wanted to came home for the weekend. She replied, "Well that's fine, dear, but your father and I won't be home Friday night because we're going out." I thought at the time how that seemed so strange, that they never went out on Friday nights, but that weekend they were gone both nights. I began to realize, belatedly, that parents have their own life! Later I said to Mother, "Your whole life is changed, without us living at home anymore, you seem to be enjoying empty-nesting." And she just said, "We've waited a long time for this."

Later in life, when I asked Dad about Mother and her priorities, he would say, "Your mother has four basic priorities: her Medicine; her children; the stock market; and me." And that's the way it was.

When I started having children, Mom told me—as though I hadn't already figured it out—she didn't really like babies very much. She liked people. When they started having a personality, that's when she could relate to them. Therefore she provided both Suzie and me with a nurse for a month after each of her grandchildren was born. She never came to visit until the grandchildren were at least three or four months old. Dad always knew exactly what to expect. It was indeed an interesting relationship, and amazingly successful.

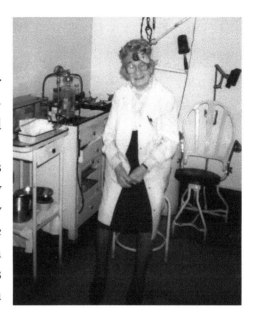

Mother, 1990-91

During my years at Brearley, my best, and only really personal and private time with my mother—when I could just talk about whatever came to mind as a teenager—was always in the evenings when Mom was in the bathtub. I'd come into the bathroom and just sit and talk.

Mother loved a deep, hot bath every night, and that's when we would discuss together whatever we wished. She would ask questions, I would ask questions, and that's how I really got to know her as a person. Mother always ended her bath with a cold shower. That was her style—not mine!

When Suzie and I were little we had the same routine every night: a bath ending with a short cold shower, whether we felt we needed it or not. One night I just didn't want a bath, saying I wasn't dirty. Out of frustration, I took off my clothes and rolled down the long hall, which had no rugs, in order to get some dirt on me. Mother just laughed and said, "Did that make you feel better?"

Some years later, when I was ten years old, I finally said, "Mother, I am ten years old, and I am never going to take another cold shower." I expected an argument. She just smiled and said, "Ok." Mother had a way, throughout my life, of arguing with me, discussing things, pushing her feelings, but whenever I was absolutely positive and sure of something, she always looked pleased.

One other important part of those Gramercy Park years, on Sunday mornings, Dad would take Suzie and me to Sunday School at Calvary Church. Located on 277 Park Avenue South at 21st street, it was within walking distance for us, and the two of us could come home by ourselves. The streets were deemed safe in those days.

Sunday mornings, for Mother, was her time to totally unwind. She would sleep in, and Dad would bring her breakfast in bed. By the time Suzie and I got home from church, Mother would still be reading the morning paper.

In the winters we would spend the rest of Sundays at home together. In the spring and fall we would go out to Far Hills for weekends.

An Early Sisterly Observation

Suzie and I had always shared a room, and I thought we were pretty much alike. One Sunday, when we were around seven and nine years old, we came home from Sunday school and Mom and Dad asked what we'd learned. That day we had been told to sit quietly and listen for God to speak to us—Calvary was a progressive church for those days. Suzie announced that God had nothing to say to her, but I reported that he had told me to be a good girl and always work hard.

Not too long ago, Suzie told me that she had mistakenly thought her teacher, who had a thick brogue accent, had said "God is gone"—rather than actually saying "God is good."

I think that little episode may have influenced her whole approach to religion—a subject upon which we have long disagreed.

Brearley School

At the end of my sixth grade year, Mother told me I was not going back to Friends Seminary. I had been enrolled in the Brearley School, which was located up on 610 East 83rd Street, right on the East River. Founded in 1885, "when it was commonly thought that intellectual activity 'took the bloom from ladies'," its first headmaster, Samuel A. Brearley, Jr., "opened the school to provide young women with an education comparable to that available to their brothers."[3]

I think that day was the only time in my life I had a tantrum. I ran to my bedroom, threw myself on the bed, and set to kicking the headboard with my feet—*and crying*! (I did take my shoes off, first.)

After a little while, Mother came in and said, "You might as well stop that. It's not going to do you any good. You're going to Brearley School." She looked at me with her kindest smile, adding, "And you'll like it."

"I won't!"

"Oh, yes you will."

The next fall, off I went to Brearley.

I repeated the sixth grade, because I was a little young, and the "powers that be" decided I would fit in better. I was always grateful for that decision. As it turned out, the grade ahead of me was not as interesting as mine. The friends I made there were just wonderful! It was a great experience, grades six through twelve.

Mother's rationale was two-fold. First, the reason for changing me to Brearley School was that she felt the girls-to-boys ratio (recall that my sixth grade class had 4 girls and twelve boys) was not ideal, even if it might change some over the years. Second, and probably more importantly, at Friends Seminary I was getting straight A's! My mother thought I needed more of an academic challenge. Mother, of course, was right. Mother was always right. I never got straight A's at Brearley, and I never knew anyone who did. It was then and it still is today one of the best academic prep schools in the country. It was just the right school for me, from start to finish.

---

3   Brearley School History Page, https://www.brearley.org/about/our-mission--history

One of my early memories of Brearley—but not a positive one—was of meeting Dr. Benjamin Spock. He was a well-known pediatrician in New York City, famous in later years for the book he wrote on raising children. *Baby and Child Care*, published in 1946, became the childcare encyclopedia for the post-war generation of new mothers.

Dr. Spock was our school doctor at the time, and he met with all new students. I was a new sixth grader, and as I walked into his office I was struck by how tall and stern-looking he was. He checked out my eyes, ears, nose and throat. But what I really recall about he was that his deep voice was scary and hands were *freezing*, all of which left me unimpressed!

Dad drove me to school the first year at Brearley, even though it was a big chore for him, because then he had to go back downtown to work.

The following year Suzie joined me at Brearley, and we moved up to 430 East 86th Street, between York and First Avenue. We walked to school and back every day, about five blocks. (Mom and Dad lived in that wonderful apartment for 67 years, until mother moved to Seattle in 1993.)

We got to school at 8:30 in the morning and arrived back home at 5:00 at night—it was a full day. Classes, study hours, lunch, athletics, and electives. There were two floors of gyms. Back then the school was ten stories high. (In the last couple decades they've added two additional floors.)

We also went on field trips. My earliest recollection of the sixth grade was studying Greek mythology. One day we were taken to the Metropolitan Museum Of Art. My teacher, Mrs. Fry, was a little woman who wore her hair back in a bun and great big glasses. She was a wonderful teacher, enthusiastic about her subject.

While at the museum that day, I was moving around too quickly in my excitement, and I bumped into a glass-enclosed little vase. The vase toppled over and fell apart! I will *never* forget that. Even then, I thought, *oh, my Gosh!* Mrs. Fry came up to me standing there in shock, and she made some remark about "Well that's going to be a little hard for your parents." I knew exactly what she was talking about. This was going to cost a lot of money—well, actually, I found out later, it was a reproduction, and it fell apart the way it had been made, and they put it back together again. It was certainly a lesson to me how not to move around a museum. I've never forgotten that day and the feeling I had seeing that vase lying there in pieces inside its little display case.

At the beginning of sixth grade, I didn't know anyone in the school, in my class. And girls at twelve and thirteen can be pretty cliquish.

The first week I was given a seat at the back of the room. We all had wooden desks with slanted tops. The teacher stood at the front of the class. I didn't know anybody, but I quickly realized there were two class leaders. One girl, Eenie Schwartz, was very blond and little. The other, Nancy Pike, was taller and her hair had the most gorgeous cork-screw brown curls just over her shoulders. They were the leaders of the class's two "gangs." I just watched for a while and thought: How am I ever going to make friends here?

We had lunch in the cafeteria every day, and then we went up to the gym where we were made to lie down on mats for twenty minutes, to "properly digest our lunches." Then we'd play for the rest of the hour in the gym. The game of the year was *dodge ball*. There were two teams at Brearley. You were either a Red or a White; and you were appointed "for life" to one of them. After lunch, in sixth grade, however, it didn't make any difference. At that point, Nancy and Eenie each had their own team.

I had played dodge ball at Friends Seminary, and I knew how to play and was pretty quick. The second day, I don't remember which team leader chose me, but I was the last one chosen both days because nobody knew me. That second day, I won for my team; I was the last one who never got hit by the ball. And from that day on, I never felt like an outsider again. I was very conscious of the fact that this was the way it was, and, if you were good at dodge ball in the sixth grade, why, you were ok. (So, after two weeks I felt completely accepted.) People made an effort to talk to me, and I made friends. Three of my best friends in the world are from Brearley and are still, fortunately, alive, living on the East Coast, and we talk two or three times a year, and I visit them occasionally.

The Brearley faculty were all strong women, dedicated teachers, and, with stylish firmness, they were capable of handling teenage girls. There was only one man. He taught shop, an elective you could choose to take in the afternoon. I loved shop, making things out of wood, learning to use a lathe, staining and polishing. I made a pair of bookends for my father, which he dutifully kept on his bureau until the day he died.

I loved athletics. Though what we could do was limited, because we couldn't be outside. We played basketball, and we

also played a variation of indoor softball which was challenging. I wasn't a superb athlete, but I was a good one. One of the things I was most proud of was in field and track, my ability to do high jump. In those days, you ran up to the high jump bar, but you didn't flip over in a backward roll or a forward roll; rather, you just kick one leg up and your other leg followed. We weren't getting as high as kids do today. I was five three or four, there at Brearley, but I was hitting almost five feet, which was very exciting! (Maybe that's why I'm suffering from arthritis in my old age— never mind—it was worth it!) We had "field days" once a year out in one of the New York city suburbs. We would have real races outside, and baseball. It was a treat!

The other athletic program I loved was tennis. Across the street from the school there were three tennis courts, part of a private club, and we were allowed to play tennis there. (It's no longer there; a great big condo complex has replaced it.) I had learned to play tennis in Far Hills with my family, and I was good enough to make the team.

In the afternoons, we had the opportunity to choose an elective. We did a lot of Gilbert and Sullivan. I especially loved "Ruddigore," in which I played Dame Hannah. Most everyone was a soprano, and I was an alto. Therefore, I got wonderful parts like Katisha in Mikado. I always got to play the parts of the deep-voiced and rather large women. Occasionally, I even had to be stuffed with a pillow.

STUDENT GOVERNMENT

First row left to right: PITT, SCHERMERHORN, BELCHER, WAINWRIGHT, BOYD
Second row left to right: COLEMAN, BELCHER, POTTER, *President*, SCHWARZ, CARTER, MILLER
Third row left to right: LEE, PATON, BROWN, MICHAELSON, HAMBRO, TOMPKINS, GATES, MARTIN

We used to be bad,
Made our teachers all mad,
Were Student Government's bane;
But our august new head
Made us good instead,
We'll never be naughty again.

The rules were unchanged,
But a means was arranged
To make all offenders lament:
To keep rules in her mind,
The offender defined,
In an essay, what our system meant.

We all realize
That it's something we prize,
Dependent on each girl's will;
Right now it's quite strong,
And it won't be so long
Before all disturbance is nil.

We had a wonderful teacher. It was a great experience practicing for months, and then having two or three performances. Our parents came. It was a highlight of the year. It was a part of an excellent education—we were very fortunate.

I also got involved in student government. I was quite serious in those days—really, right into high school—and I frowned a lot. Mother told me, if I didn't stop frowning, I would have lines in my forehead by the time I was forty. (It took a little longer than that.) In the eighth grade I was a "prefect."

There were school rules, two of which were followed very strictly. One, you couldn't talk in the elevator. This rule was strongly enforced because the woman running the elevator had to be able to hear when someone called out their floor, which would be very difficult if you had twelve girls in there talking at the same time.

The other rule: you couldn't run in the hall. And if you ran in the hall—the halls were long—you could be cited.

One of my best friends, Eenie, the little blond girl who led one of the two sixth grade gangs, loved being naughty. She thought student government was "for the birds."

Well, I had to report her—*twice*! It was fine with her. She had to come up before student government. If you had more than one citation, the punishment was to memorize part of the Constitution. By the time those of us who sat on student government finished our terms of office, we, too, had learned much of the Constitution, because we'd heard it recited so many times.

Early on in my eighth grade student government experience, I came home one day really distressed. I had had to report Eenie yet another time, and she had to go to the "upper school" student government because she continued to ignore the rules. When I got home I realized I had scratched my forehead to the point of drawing blood, I was so frustrated. Mother came into my room and exclaimed, "What are you doing?" I shook my head, looking at the blood on my hand and replied, "I'm just so upset!"

So, I got a long lecture from Mom on how one handled situations, and how, if one was going to take on responsibility, one would need to learn to be objective about it. After what she said to me, I never again, in such a situation, felt it was my fault.

The upper school was very challenging, intellectually and academically. It was tough! But we learned to write well; and for those days, we had labs which were superb. I studied English literature, physics, and biology. I did four years of Latin, which was one of my favorite subjects, and four years of math. We also had a great course in United States History.

French was my least favorite subject. Thanks to our French governesses, I had learned to speak the language well, and actually to read French also. But I'd never had to learn grammar, and in the French course at school, the grammar was terribly important. I hated it, it didn't make any sense to me, and Madam "C" despaired of teaching me.

All in all, Brearley School was a wonderful experience. The friends I made there are still good friends to this day. Above all, we were taught that anything was possible and many of us believed that the world was waiting for us!

When we were seniors we began thinking of college. We were all expected to go to college. In those days there weren't many co-ed colleges, and many of the students from Brearley had always gone to Bryn Mawr College. There was a relationship between the two schools, as our Head, Mrs. MacIntosh, had been Dean at Bryn Mawr before coming to Brearley.

Some went to Vassar, some went to Smith, some to Wellesley. These were the main colleges called the Seven Sisters Schools. The others were Mount Holyoke, Barnard, and Radcliffe.

Occasionally, someone would go across the country to Mills college in California.

With my best friend Dory Gates, I visited Vassar for a weekend, and stayed with some upper class girls whom we knew. We did the same at Smith College and Bryn Mawr. Both Dory and I decided Smith was the best place. We liked the girls there, they were so enthusiastic, and we thought the campus was wonderful. My friends said, "Oh, you're not going to Bryn Mawr, because you're not smart enough." So, I asked Mother and Dad to pay the entrance fee to see if I could get into Bryn Mawr, along with Smith. I was accepted to both.

Diane Guggenheim

My years at the Brearley School were fascinating in many ways, not the least of which was the fact that quite a few of my friends came from very interesting families, some of whom were very different from mine. Occasionally I got to spend a weekend with one of these families.

One of my most memorable weekends was spent with Diane Guggenheim, daughter of Harry Frank Guggenheim (1890–1971). Diane was a little younger than I, and we became friends. Two or three times she invited me to spend the weekend with her at her father's home on Long Island Sound. He had built a beautiful mansion in the style of an English manor house and named it "Falaise." It was an unbelievable estate.

That particular spring weekend, we went down to Falaise on a Friday afternoon and were driven by the chauffeur back to Brearley on Sunday. I was about 16 at the time, and I brought my tennis racket with me. Diane didn't play tennis, but occasionally I would play tennis with her father when he had other guests and needed a fourth.

We arrived and were met by the chef, whom I called the chief of staff. Somehow, he was always out waiting for us by the front door. He was a great big man, in total, spotless white with a great big chef's hat. Curiously, the man had no eyebrows; I speculated this condition was probably due to bending over too many hot stoves for too many years. He was a wonderful cook and great fun, welcoming us into the kitchen anytime we wanted anything or just wanting to talk.

That weekend, shortly after we arrived, Mr. Guggenheim—who had a friend with him—said,

Kate with Toby, Suzie with Kris, Dad & Mom (1942)

"Kate, would you like to play tennis?" I said, "Sure." So Mr. Guggenheim introduced his friend, whose name I didn't catch. The man looked old to me, maybe late fifties, white hair, not tall, though well-built. We went out to the tennis courts and I beat him in the first set, six–four. The man looked at me and said, "Would you like to play another set?" I said, "Yes, I'd like to." So we played another set, and again I beat him six–four. As we were walking back to the house, he asked, "Are you a student of theater?" I said, "Well, I love to go to the theater, and to Broadway shows, but I have no acting talent to speak of and really no desire to get into that side of life. I just enjoy being a spectator." He said, almost to himself, "I thought so."

After we got back to the house, I went up to my room to change my clothes. Diane came in the room, and I asked her, "Who was that man I was playing tennis with?" She answered, "Oh, that was George Abbott." George Francis Abbott (1887–1995) was one of the best known directors and producers of plays on Broadway. So, I told Diane what had happened on the tennis court, and we had a big laugh. Obviously, Mr. Abbott had thought I would let him win because I likely would want something from the famous Broadway producer.

The Brearley Reading List

The "Brearley School Minimum List of Novels Every Girl Should Read Before She Finishes Class XII" is now 75 years old. I wonder if a graduating senior today has ever heard of many of these classics—excepting maybe for those that have been made into popular movies.

THE BREARLEY SCHOOL

KHB-1942

1.

Minimum List of Novels Every Girl Should Read

Before She Finishes Class XII

(No time is allowed in school for this reading)

Pride and Prejudice	Jane Austen
The Old Wives' Tale	Arnold Bennett
Lorna Doone	R. D. Blackmore
Jane Eyre	Charlotte Brontë
Wuthering Heights	Emily Brontë
The Last Days of Pompeii	Edward Bulwer-Lytton
The Pilgrim's Progress	John Bunyan
Evelina	Fanny Burney
Huckleberry Finn	Samuel L. Clemens (Mark Twain)
Tom Sawyer	
Lord Jim	Joseph Conrad
Youth	
The Last of the Mohicans	James Fenimore Cooper
The Red Badge of Courage	Stephen Crane
Robinson Crusoe	Daniel Defoe
David Copperfield	Charles Dickens
Pickwick Papers	
A Tale of Two Cities	

Minimum List of Novels Every Girl Should Read

Before She Finishes Class XII

The Mill on the Floss	George Eliot
Tom Jones	Henry Fielding
The Forsyte Saga	John Galsworthy
The Vicar of Wakefield	Oliver Goldsmith
Far From the Madding Crowd	Thomas Hardy
The Return of the Native	
The House of the Seven Gables	Nathaniel Hawthorne
The Scarlet Letter	
Les Miserables	Victor Hugo
The American	Henry James
Daisy Miller	
Westward Ho !	Charles Kingsley
Captains Courageous	Rudyard Kipling
Kim	
Moby Dick	Herman Melville
The Ordeal of Richard Feverel	George Meredith
The Cloister and the Hearth	Charles Reade
Ivanhoe	Sir Walter Scott
Kenilworth	

3.

Minimum List of Novels Every Girl Should Read
Before She Finishes Class XII

Treasure Island	Robert Louis Stevenson
Gulliver's Travels	Jonathan Swift
Henry Esmond	William Makepeace Thackeray
Vanity Fair	
War and Peace	Leo Tolstoi
Barchester Towers	Anthony Trollope
The Age of Innocence	Edith Wharton

Two or three volumes of Short Stories

chosen from the collected work of the

following authors:

Ambrose Bierce, John Galsworthy, Katherine Mansfield,

Bret Harte, Rudyard Kipling, H. H. Munro (Saki),

William Sidney Porter (O. Henry), James Stephens,

Robert Louis Stevenson.

Sunnybranch, Lo-An-Oak, Far Hills, New Jersey

"Ah, to be in Far Hills when autumn comes again!"[1]

From the time I was born, until I graduated from Smith College, I spent every summer of my life in Far Hills, New Jersey, at my Grandmother Belcher's home. Originally, my grandparents lived in a home they called Sunnybranch. After that was sold in the early 1900s, they bought and moved to what they named Lo-An-Oak, two hundred acres upon which the only tree of any significance was a vast and beautiful oak.

An unforgettable family story described the way my grandfather, Zachariah Belcher IV, "Fafa," found water on the property. Holding in his hands a forked, y-shaped witch hazel dowsing stick parallel to the ground, Fafa walked around waiting for the end of the stick to dip down. The belief was that this "divining rod," when pointing downward, would indicate the presence of potable water. Fafa was a believer, and it worked for him. Enough water was discovered to service the entire family and a large dairy farm for more than a century. My grandfather had a windmill built and the tower held the pure, cold, delicious water for us all.

I was named after grandmother Kate Helena Fuller Belcher. Zachariah Belcher IV and Kate Helena married on 10 November 1886. My mother, Anne Mae Seligman, married my father Harold Stewart Belcher on 27 December 1922, in Newark, New Jersey.

My grandmother and grandfather had built Lo-An-Oak in the early 20th century. It was a great big house, with ten bedrooms for family and four bedrooms for the "help." There was also a cottage, less than a quarter mile down the road from the house, which originally was the superintendent's cottage. My mother and father, Aunt Mary and Uncle Charlie Ashmun, along with their three boys, Charles "Chil," George "Geo," and John, my Uncle Spike and his daughter Blanche, and grandmother "Nana" all lived together in the Big House every summer. (My Grandfather, who died when I was six, always insisted we all will live under one roof.)

Dad's oldest brother, my uncle Malcolm (James Malcolm Belcher), and his wife Llda, whom we called "Dubby," and their three children, Jim, Russ, and Mary lived in the cottage.

Malcolm had been the only child of my grandparents to fight in World War I. He was wounded quite severely in France, rendering his left arm permanently stiff. After the war he lived in New York with his wife and first child. He worked there and hated it. After a few months

he came home to Far Hills and asked his father if he could live in the superintendent's house and start a dairy farm. He worked the farm quite successfully, with a prize herd of Jersey cows. We were brought up on unpasteurized, very rich, Jersey cow milk with the cream on top of the bottle. It was *nummy*, except for the spring when onions sprouted all over the fields—then the milk tasted awful!

Malcolm also served as the mayor of Far Hills for thirty-seven years. He was born in 1887 and died in 1987, living to be a hundred and a few months, always kind and curious.

In the Big House, as we called it, every family lived in a separate section. Mother and Dad, Suzie and I got the back end of the house to ourselves. Suzie and I had adjoining bedrooms and shared a bathroom with our parents. My room was right next to the back stairs, a small winding set of wooden steps which went down to the kitchen, the pantry, the maids dining room, the laundry room and the icebox room.

Perhaps because I was so close to that part of the house, I got to befriend all the house-staff. Before the war, we always had a cook; the one I came to know best was Nellie. She was German and wore high-button shoes. She showed me how to button them with a button-hook. She was always very patient with me, about answering my continuous questions, and in the kitchen she always let me lick the bowl after making something yummy.

When I was eight years old, we had a French governess named Anna. Coincidentally, nearly all our governesses were named Anna. The Ashmun boys had a German governess named Sophie, and my cousin Blanche had a governess named Peggy. Blanche also had a Scotty dog which was named Peggy. So it was Peggy the Margaret and Peggy the dog.

Nana, my grandmother, never drove. She always had a chauffeur to drive her Pierce Arrow automobile, until wartime. Hughie was the estate chauffeur I recall best, when I was seven or eight, and he stayed with us the longest. His name was Hugh, and he was Irish. He worked for Grandmother up until he was called to war.

There was another maid, Katherine; she was the downstairs maid.

One of the things we were not supposed to do, which I learned early on, was to visit the maids' dining room when they were eating their supper. Nana considered that their private time, not to be bothered by the family. I was very curious about this injunction. One time I asked Nellie, the cook, who was the unspoken boss of all the "help," if I could come and sit in the rocking chair in the corner of the maids dining room if I didn't say a word but just sat quietly. She said, "Yes, if you don't tell anybody."

I did just that for a couple of summers. It was like a United Nations, with the Germans and the Irish and the French. The all seemed mostly to get along, though there were some arguments as well. For me, it was an education.

At Far Hills, as a child, the routine was prescribed. We knew what was happening at any given time or day. Breakfast in the morning same time every day, between 8:00 and 8:30. We had lunch with Grandmother at noon, during the week. All of the parents were gone to their various jobs, working during the day. Therefore, it was Nana and the six of us kids: Suzie and me, Chil,

33

Geo and Johnny Ashmun, and Blanche Belcher. Between my sister, the youngest, and cousin Charlie (Chil), the oldest, we ranged across ten years.

We all sat down at the dining room table with Nana for, what she called, "very good conversation time." One day a week, we were to speak only French. Some of the French phrases became second nature to us, for example, our favorite, *"J'ai bien peur de me perdre en route"* ("I am afraid I shall lose my way"). We also laughed a lot. And there were lessons, too!

Lesson number one: All our vegetables came from Uncle Malcolm's garden. One day at lunch we had a big salad. All of a sudden I saw a little green worm on my plate. I couldn't help myself. I said, "Oooo! There's a worm!" Nana said, "My dear, in that case, cover it up and get on with your meal. We do not comment on things like that at the table."

Lesson number two: I was a chocoholic, and in those days (and still today) chocolate cake was my favorite. One day we had chocolate cake for dessert, along with fruit. Katherine, the downstairs maid, was passing the cake around for seconds. There was only one piece left when she got to me, and there was still my cousin Johnny after me. Of course, I took the piece of cake. Nana said, "Kate, John might have wanted that." I said, "But I came first." Though she was always partial to the boys, she had to laugh!

(Not too many years ago, I talked about that funny incident with cousin Johnny, and he still remembered it.)

There was one bittersweet memory related to those luncheons: It was 1936. We were all sitting there having a wonderful time, laughing about something. Cousin Geo Ashmun got up from the table and started walking around the table, as if he was an old man walking with a cane, and said, "I have something to say." None of us knew what was coming. Geo always had the light touch; he was the cousin who made everybody laugh. He said, in an old man voice, "I think that in the year 2000 we should have a family reunion. Who knows where we'll all be by then. Ok?" Then he sat down, and we all agreed "great idea!"

Strangely enough, none of us ever forgot Geo's idea. Toward the end of the 1990s, we began to send letters and emails asking "What about our 2000 anniversary reunion?"

Indeed, we did just that in 2000, right here at Sunnybranch on Bainbridge Island, sixty-four years later. (See page 134 and following.)

There were 52 of us, three generations. We all toasted, remembered and honored cousin Geo, who was killed in World War II.

As we got older, the Ashmun boys spent their days helping Uncle Malcolm in the fields. They would drive the tractor, help bring in the hay, work in the barn. Blanche, Suzie and I worked in the house. I learned how to cut and arrange flowers. Grandmother taught me hospital corners when making beds and how to clean bathrooms. There were many household tasks learned that summer that I never expected to use. To my great surprise, they were important skills to rely on as the years went by.

The other thing Nana did, and this was incredible as I look back at it: The three youngest of the group, Suzie, Johnny, and I all took piano lessons in the wintertime. Nana had been trained as a concert pianist when she was young and was still a skilled musician. In the summertime, five days a week, Nana would sit down for one hour with each one of us to practice. She would talk about what we were doing and teach us all about music. These were special moments with Nana, which we all remember. Once a week we each would also have a "lesson" from Aunt Peg Squibb. She taught us Wagner's main themes in his "Ring Cycle." (To this day I can recognize many of them.)

On Sundays, after early church services, we would come home, and play tennis or croquet or perhaps help Mom weed her garden.

Sunday afternoon was always family music time. At Lo-An-Oak, my grandfather had added a room to the Big House, which became known as the music room. You walked into it down five steps. It was a huge space with marvelous acoustics! There was a great big bay window, two grand pianos, a pump organ, a fireplace, and lots of comfy seats. Over the organ was an elegant, art nouveau stained-glass window created by a first cousin of my Grandfather. (It now hangs in the master bathroom at Sunnybranch, Bainbridge Island.)

Uncle Malcolm would play the organ while Grandmother played one piano, Dad played the violin, Uncle Spike played the cello, and Aunt Mary played the second piano or led in the singing. There would be classical music for a while, and then we would get out all the old sheet music and play and sing the popular tunes of the day: "Brother, Can You Spare A Dime"; "Five Foot Two, Eyes Of Blue"; "Stormy Weather." We enjoyed lots of Irving Berlin and Cole Porter.

When I was at Brearley, Dory Gates was my best friend. Her family had a summer home up at Woods Hole, Massachusetts. Her parents had built the house in 1927. From the time I was twelve until the war, when I was eighteen, I spent almost a month on Cape Cod every summer visiting Dory and two other friends who lived on the Cape. This was where I learned to sail. My love of the sea began there. Other than those wonderful times spent at the Cape, my summers were primarily spent at Far Hills.

I learned years later that one of the reasons we were hustled out of New York City off to Far Hills, from the day school stopped to the day before school started up in the fall, was because of Polio. There was just a lot of it in those days. Dad and Mom thought it best if we got out of the City, and, of course, it provided us with a wonderful summer with our extended family.

Uncle Malcolm's farm was a major part of Lo-An-Oak, but another important feature was the clay tennis court. Every Saturday morning, Dad, Uncle Spike, and the boys—as they got older—watered and rolled the clay court and put on new lines of wet lime. This was so that the court would always be in shape for weekend play. We all learned to play tennis on that court. The whole family played. Mother, who was not a bit athletic, got me out there for one whole summer early on—I was probably eight or nine at the
time—and she taught me the basics. Dad helped too, and then Mother and I would play a set. The day I beat Mother, when I was ten, was the day she said to Dad, "Ok, you take over now. And get the boys to help." So I grew up playing tennis with my older cousins and have always loved the game.

There are many stories from the Far Hills time of my life. When I was thirteen, my Uncle Malcolm said to me, "Would you like to learn to drive the tractor?" "Oh, yes!" I answered. So, right there, he taught me how to drive the tractor.

We started with going up and down the road. A few days later, it was time to start picking up the hay. We didn't have a hay baler, or one of those racks that picked up the mown hay mechanically and rolled it up into the wagon. We packed the cut alfalfa onto the wagon behind the tractor. The boys followed the tractor-pulled wagon and loaded hay with pitchforks into the wagon. Uncle Malcolm said, "Why don't you drive the tractor and pull the hay wagon today." What an exciting experience that was!

I was having a wonderful time driving the tractor, when all of a sudden I heard yelling behind me. I stopped and called out, "What's the matter?" Uncle Malcolm called back, "Stop racing! You're going too fast, and we can't keep up with you as we pick up the hay." From that I earned one of my nicknames, "old lead-foot."

Just being part of that rural life made me feel I could do my share, too, and be part of the "crew."

A little later that summer, I learned to drive the tractor, back and forth, in front of the barn. The hay wagon would be parked in the barn with a fork on a track above. The fork would then take a big hunk of hay and pull it up and drop it into the hayloft. I became very adept at driving the tractor—at least I thought so.

Around that time, when I was twelve or thirteen, on Sundays I used to go down to the cottage where Uncle Malcolm and Aunt Dubby lived, along with their children, Jim, Russ, and Mary. I loved watching Uncle Malcolm get dinner ready; they always had a big Sunday dinner about an hour before we did (at the Big House up the hill), and he was always the cook. They had either roast beef or a big roast chicken. In those days one roast chicken really did feed a whole family—they were a lot bigger than chickens are today, especially if they came from Uncle Malcolm's barn.

On one particular day, it was a roast beef Sunday and Uncle Malcolm was making gravy in the pan after taking the beef out to rest. Half-way through, he turned to me and said, "Kate, you may be a little young for this, but I want you to remember: Never make gravy after you have had anything to drink, because it won't taste the same." He was right. And I have always remembered his excellent advice.

In Far Hills, the dinners we had during wartime were noisy and unpredictable; we never knew whether there would be five or twelve of us dining on any given evening. Some family members commuted, and at different times through the summer some of the boys would arrive home for a short "leave." Nana was always at the head of the table, and whoever else attended would be sprinkled around as they arrived. There were no formal seating assignments, although each of us had our own silver napkin-ring, and it was a challenge to find our own napkin.

There was always a lot of chit-chat at the table, and every once in a while a great argument would ensue about heaven-knows-what. Such "discussions" were mostly about ideas, literature, people, rather than arguments about current events at the time.

One evening, the conversation became rather loud and raucous. Uncle Gayle—who had married Aunt Mary after Uncle Charles' death and had a very deep and commanding voice—raised his hands and said simply, "SUNT!" Everyone turned and looked at him as though he'd lost his mind. None of us knew what he was talking about. Uncle Gayle continued, "We need to find a way to stop this kind of arguing. There is an old Latin saying, *De gustibus non est disputandum*, which literally means 'there is no disputing about tastes'." There would be no way to get that phrase out in order to disrupt any kind of a heated conversation or argument. Therefore one would simply use the word 'sunt' (which is the third person plural pronoun in the Latin). Translation: "we agree to disagree."

After Uncle Gayle had delivered that evening his dissertation on "SUNT," we all sat there in stunned silence. Everyone concluded it was a pretty good idea.

From that day to the present, at various Belcher dinners or gatherings, when heated disputation or arguments develop, someone inevitably raises their hand and says, "SUNT!" And that's the end of it.

For Mom's and Dad's fiftieth wedding anniversary, my sister had made a pillow for them; in needle-point, she had put on it a great big red heart and, in white letters, the word "SUNT." We still have that pillow, and it makes me smile every time I look at it.

In the summer in Jersey, it often got very hot. When we were teenagers, sometimes we would go up to bed, lie in our various rooms in the heat, and someone would call out, "Let's go swimming!"

We didn't have a swimming pool. But our neighbors down the road, the Dillons, did. We had the tennis court, they had the swimming pool. Our families were close friends; they had three boys in their family. So, on a long hot night, when someone said, "Let's go swimming," we all piled into one of the station wagons and Chil drove us to the Dillons' place.

There was a great high wooden stake fence around the pool, eight feet high. The gate was always locked. We were very quiet. One of the boys climbed over fence, unlocked the gate, and we all jumped in the pool. The Dillons kept their pool at around fifty-five degrees, and it felt cold. It was cold! We lasted maybe ten minutes. Cooled off, we rushed back home. I don't think we really fooled anybody, but we were never "caught."

As my freshman year at Smith drew to a close, many of my classmates who had decided to spend the summer working at farms in Connecticut Valley. There was a great shortage of "pickers" due to the war, and we all thought this summer work could be our contribution to the war effort.

I wrote Mother and Dad about my plans. They both wrote back by return mail that indeed that was not where I was going to spend my summer! I had never received letters from both of them at the same time before, so this singular event impressed me. They both made a strong case against my working at a farm, and therefore I changed my plans.

The family, Mom and Dad, Aunts and Uncles, and Nana had decided that Blanche, who had been running the "Big House" at Lo-An-Oak for two years needed a break.

I was the next in line for the job. It was with a considerable amount of trepidation that I packed up and headed for Far Hills and a whole new experience.

Kate In The Kitchen

On Monday morning, Nana sat me down and outlined my duties. For breakfast, everyone was on their own. I was to have coffee, bread, cereal and juice all prepared; and I would clean the kitchen after everyone had finished eating.

Katherine, the "downstairs maid," was the only staff remaining at Lo-An-Oak. Her job was to set the table and wash all the dishes, silverware, and glasses. She also did some dusting and vacuum cleanup of the downstairs.

It was my job to make sure the bathrooms were clean, and towels and washcloths were changed regularly. Bed sheets, along with white damask (dinner) tablecloths, were sent out for laundering. But I learned how to wash the large white damask napkins, and iron them with heavy irons heated on the wood stove. Part of my job was also to keep fresh flowers in the dining room, living rooms, and Nana's bedroom. There were plenty of flowers to pick from Malcolm's garden or Mom's flowerbed. Mother spent every weekend tending her flowers and they were lovely.

The big deal for me was the cooking! On that first Monday discussion with Nana, I told her that scrambled eggs and fudge were all I could cook. "How am I going to survive?" I asked. Nana said, "You can read, can't you?" Upon my assent, she pointed to the cook books in the kitchen and said, "We'll discuss weekly menus and you'll do just fine." And that is what we did.

I loved the kitchen and really enjoyed the challenge.

I provided meals for a bunch of "strong individuals." My relatives were an outspoken group, and there was no way to please everyone at any given meal. When I complained about that to Nana, she gave me an answer I've never forgotten: "My dear," she said, "if the plates are hot when they should be hot and cold when they should be cold and if the meal is served on time, you don't have to worry about anything else."

Preparing lunch was fairly easy, because there were seldom more than five or six us at the table. Dinners were more difficult. I often never knew how many there would be seated until late in the afternoon. The numbers varied between five and a dozen. We always had soup, meat, potatoes, vegetables, and dessert. Then demitasse on the porch. Somehow it all worked out.

Train Station, Far Hills, New Jersey

Zach, Harold, Mal

Picking Fruit, Far Hills

My Uncle Malcolm, whom we called "Mal," was a huge help. Most of the vegetables, berries, cherries, peaches and apples came from his farm—as well as milk (unpasteurized), eggs and butter. He would watch me pick the vegetables and would often say, "That's not enough." He was usually right, so I would go on picking as he directed.

At one point, my uncles and my father decided it would be a good time for me to learn about drinking. I was 19 and had already learned about Rum and Coca-Cola and beer at college, but they thought I needed to understand the world of "cocktails." The first week they offered one daiquiri before dinner; the next week, in not too small glasses, they allowed two drinks, and I could still manage to get dinner on the table. But when they insisted I have three glasses—all of which tasted wonderful!—that was my downfall. They sent me to bed. The next day they all congratulated me

The Big House at Far Hills

and said not to forget that two drinks was always enough. Good advice that still holds true.

That summer gave me a unique three months of new experiences, responsibilities and extraordinary opportunities to know my grandmother as a mentor, but also as a friend. I would drive her to market, the hair salon and to church, and best of all to have tea with friends. I was full of questions about everything and she was extremely patient and thoughtful with answers. Nana was an extraordinary woman. She never raised her voice, but she always knew what she wanted, and somehow life went her way.

The Barn at Lo-An-Oak, Far Hills

Grandmother Kate Helena Fuller Belcher

An extraordinary, talented, gracious and digni-
fied woman, Kate Helena Fuller Belcher (1854–
1949) could spend an afternoon entertaining a
rowdy yet beloved bunch of grandchildren, or
entertaining a group of beautifully-gowned and
coiffed ladies to tea, or spend a day at "The Clinic"
keeping track of the New Jersey Planned Parenthood organization (of which she was a founder,
and its first president in 1927).

Her ability to handle any situation with firmness and serenity was always a source of amaze-
ment to us. Kate Helena Fuller Belcher was a
grand role model to learn from and remember!

Sunnybranch, c. 1895. Top: Harold, Kate, Mary.
Bottom: Zach, Zachariah, Malcolm

Planned Parenthood

IN NEW JERSEY

SPRING, 1945

EIGHTEEN YEARS AGO

In March, April and May, back in the year 1927, a series of informal meetings were held in the homes of prominent Newark women. Usually Miss Henrietta Hart, who was to become New Jersey's first executive secretary with the Planned Parenthood organization, was there to spur things on and Mrs. Zachariah Belcher, who became the first president, usually presided with graciousness and dignity. Indeed many women were first won by Mrs. Belcher's quiet sincerity, long before they studied the cause she espoused. There were other pioneers in that small but effective group. - Miss Jessie P. Condit, director of the Children's Society, Dr. Wells P. Eagleton and his understanding wife and Dr. Sara P. Smalley, fresh from a New York internship.

In the archives of the New Jersey League for Planned Parenthood are filed, in her own careful handwriting, Mrs. Belcher's notes of a talk delivered one year later - a talk recording accomplishment with the clinic ready to open. Let us read through those carefully jotted items:

"The National League first sent us one of their field secretaries. We had parlor talks succeeded by others of the same nature where Miss H. was invited. Then on April 27 groups came together to meet Dr. Stone - a great privilege. In May an attempt was made to organize, all officers, however, serving pro tem. In June Margaret Sanger was present at a meeting in Convent attended by representatives from all the towns where contacts had been made. Then came weeks of work - educational, fund-raising, interesting the physicians, trying to show how clear and logical the plan is. And let me assure you that we have behind us not only the N. Y. State women but also a fine and large number of New Jersey people who are realizing the fundamental need of this kind of social service. It has been a personal appeal from woman to woman and many of us are only beginning to study what this movement may mean to those who have had no op. (opportunity) to learn what medical science is doing for motherhood.

"The homes we aim to reach are those where children have come so fast that there is no room for them, where mothers have no adequate knowledge of how to care for their own bodies & are often weak and unfit for what sh. (should) be their high function of motherhood - where fathers are overburdened with the hopeless struggle to provide even enough food for their families.

"Do not think that we believe that this attempt to establish maternity health centers is going to be a cure all for all human ills. We all know better than that; but when our best medical men are bringing a thoroughly scientific knowledge to the aid of suffering men and women sh. (should) we not at least face this problem of the home without prejudice, with a desire to learn how much better its problems may be met? I need not tell you how many physicians are in sympathy with this belief that by the spread of this knowledge homes can be kept happy and normal. But it is the people who have not the chance or do not know how to get scientific medical advice whom we aim to help. Those who work in the poorer districts of our country towns know people they would like to help where shall we send them?

"My vision is that in all our hospitals before long we shall be able to find a dept. especially equipped to give advice to all who have 'just cause'. But in the meantime shall we stand still and rest on the fact that that day is coming, yet never raise our hands to help? Are not all of us of the belief that women have a right to this knowledge, are we not bound to express this belief according to our opportunity?"

Eighteen years ago, yet that speech would be just as valid today when there are still many areas in our state where guidance in family planning is unavailable to those who wish it. It is true that 1,690 physicians in New Jersey have received copies of the medical text "Contraceptive Technique" and that we are constantly reaching more nurses and social workers who can direct patients to private physicians skilled in this phase of preventive medicine or to the fourteen clinics operating throughout the state. But much education is still to be done.

On the League's eighteenth birthday it seems especially fitting that we honor its far-seeing founder, Mrs. Zachariah Belcher, whose guidance and wisdom have made it possible for over 35,000 families to control their own destiny.

MRS. ZACHARIAH BELCHER
First President

EVERY CHILD

A WANTED CHILD

NEW JERSEY LEAGUE *for* PLANNED PARENTHOOD

71 LINCOLN PARK Telephone MArket 3-6139 NEWARK 2, N. J.

President
MRS. DONALD W. SINCLAIR

Treasurer
MRS. GEORGE D. SMITH

State Director
MRS. RUBY S. CAMPBELL

September 8, 1949

Dear Dr. Belcher:

It is with deep regret that the Board of the New Jersey League for Planned Parenthood has learned of the death of Mr. Zachariah Belcher.

The New Jersey Birth Control League was started at a time when a courageous and crusading spirit was needed to face the odds against the program — and we owe a tremendous debt to the farsightedness and inspiration of Mr. Belcher who was one of the founders and the first President.

The Board wishes me to express to you and your family its real regret and heartfelt sympathy. May I add my personal message to you and Dr. Anne?

Sincerely,

Edith S. Stevens

Mrs. J. P. Stevens Jr

Corresponding Secretary

PLANNED PARENTHOOD CLINICS

*ASBURY PARK: 913 Sewell Avenue
*CAMDEN: 571 Benson Street
EAST ORANGE: 143 New Street
*ELIZABETH: 1131 East Jersey Street
*ENGLEWOOD: 11 North Dean Street

*MONTCLAIR: Mountainside Hospital
*MORRISTOWN: 319 Park Square Building
MOUNT HOLLY: Burlington County Hospital
*NEWARK: 71 Lincoln Park

NEW BRUNSWICK: Middlesex General Hospital
ORANGE: Orange Memorial Hospital
*PATERSON: 95 Bridge Street
*PLAINFIELD: 703 Watchung Avenue
*TRENTON: 132 E. Hanover Street

Members of the New Jersey League for Planned Parenthood

Smith College

"In Virtue One Gains Knowledge" — Ἐν τῇ ἀρετῇ τὴν γνῶσιν

I graduated from Brearley in 1942. My four years at Smith, in Northampton, Massachusetts, were "war" years. This made the experience quite singular, socially at least, and to a degree academically. Social life at the time was not great, because most of the boys were off to war. There were some around, with the occasional weekend parties at Yale, Dartmouth, Princeton, Harvard, and our nearest neighbor Amherst.

Social life from 1942–1946 was largely in-house. We made more friends, and closer friends, and longer-lasting friends, than normally I think happens at college. This is one of the reasons I feel so grateful to have gone to Smith. I still have eight or ten very close friends all across the country, whom I can call anytime, and they instantly recognize my voice, and we have kept close and in touch all these years.

I have to say that I didn't work, i.e. study, as hard as I should have. I was having such a good time. I played soccer all four years—and tennis. Student government was a big part of my life there. Lots of warm friendships developed with both peers and faculty.

One thing I am very grateful for is that I took a wide variety of courses. Though I never got to be an expert in any single particular field, I was exposed to a lot of intellectual and academic areas that I might otherwise never have known about. I started off as a pre-med student, because I planned to be a doctor—with both Mother and Dad in medicine it seemed the natural choice. Therefore, I took pre-med for two years, which gave me more courses in physics and chemistry, and also two years of German, which in those days was a prerequisite for medical school.

At the end of those two years I decided I really didn't want a medical career badly enough. My reasoning, at nineteen years old, was that I didn't have the stamina my mother had, and couldn't see myself in that profession. Of course, that wasn't the best reasoning for this decision. (Actually, now, I think I have my mother's stamina, but back then I didn't want it badly enough to work for it. If you're going to be a doctor, especially a woman doctor, you have to want it more than anything in the world. It wasn't easy for a woman to get into medical school, nor to be a physician. So, I know that for me, at the time, it was the right decision.)

Next, I decided to be a math major. We were still at war, and I thought I would graduate with a degree in math and could contribute somehow. Not that I knew how, it just seemed math made more sense than English or history.

In my senior year we all could see the war was drawing to an end. One course I really wanted to take was called "The Bible And The Common Reader" (i.e., the Bible as literature). The instructor was Mary Ellen Chase, a writer, author, and a wonderful English professor. You had to be an English major to take this course; it was not even open to audit. It turned out I had enough extra hours to switch majors, once again. So, I graduated with a major in English, and a lot of math along the way.

Looking back, I don't regret anything. If I were a college student today, I likely would have stuck with my math major, given modern technology and the computer. The problem with math at that time was visualizing, for example, some of the more complicated kinds of geometry. Today, you can find it all on the Internet. But conceptually, at that point, it was beyond me.

The reason I had those extra hours which allowed me to switch majors from math to English is a story in itself.

During my sophomore year at Smith, one of our activities was to ride a bike over to Amherst. My roommate Candy McKee, who later married cousin Chil to become Candy Ashmun, had an aunt and uncle in Belchertown, which was just outside of Amherst. It was about a half hour bike ride from Smith to Amherst, and we used to visit to ride their horses—and incidentally enjoy great meals.

One day in May, Candy and I went over to the farm for an outing and some horseback riding. That day I was wearing shorts, and the stirrup straps rubbed and pinched both my calves.

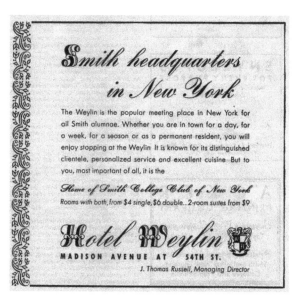

Add from the Smith Alumnae Quarterly1946.

Next day there were big bruises, which became swollen. I went to the infirmary. They didn't know what it was, and put on hot-packs. That didn't help, and my calves swelled bigger. The next day they tried cold-packs. Both blood clots started to dissolve, and you could see them traveling up my legs.

Candy and my sister Suzie were very worried and decided to call Mother to come and get me. This was war time, but Mom had gasoline because doctors were given extra rations to get it. So, my mother, and my cousin Charlie Ashmun, who was home on leave, drove up to Smith to pick me up.

Mother took one look at me and said to Chil, "Ok, carry her out to the car."

I said, "What do you mean, I have to be carried?"

Mother said, "You are not to be on your feet!"   And I said, "But I have to go to the bath-room!"

"Alright, Charlie," she replied, "take her to the bathroom."

And he did just that, waited for me, then carried me back out to the car. They took me back to New York, and I was in bed for three weeks, having been diagnosed with "phlebitis."

In those days there was no Heparin or Coumadin to thin blood.

For awhile things were uncertain, and we had to wait and see that I would be ok.

And I was.

But, as a result, I missed all my finals for my sophomore year. Therefore, I went back to Smith for summer school. During the war, Smith had developed an accelerated program. If some women wanted to get through more quickly, they could go summers and finish in three years. So, I went all summer, took my missed exams, and also some English courses. And therefore I had enough extra credits to change my major from math to English.

Wartime Debutant Party Makes The Pages Of Life Magazine

In the fall of 1942, my freshman year at Smith, Mother wrote informing me that I had been invited to a big Christmas ball in New York City. For my generation, many in their freshmen year of college "came out" as debutants. My family would never have considered a debutant party for me. But I was the right age, and had gone to the "right schools," so I was invited to be one of fifty girls to attend this party.

There were not going to be any big "private parties" during the war years.

I came home at Thanksgiving, and Mother said we needed to buy a dress. Mom never believed in spending lots of money on clothes, but this time, she said, "We'll do it right."

We went to Bonwit Teller, Saks Fifth Avenue, and ended up at Henri Bendel's, a small Fifth Avenue boutique. There we found a dress, a white lace, princessy kind of dress, fitted at the top with a full skirt. It had gold-sequined clover-leaves on it here and there. It was very pretty and cost fifty dollars. Mother said she'd never spent fifty dollars on any single piece of clothing in her life. Nonetheless, she agreed to buy it.

On the way out she said to the sales girls, "Well, there are not going to be any more of these at the party, are there?"

The woman replied, "Oh, no, of course not! We don't do that."

So it was back to college, then home again for Christmas, and then time for the Ball.

And—guess what?—there were *three* of us there wearing the very same dress! Fortunately we didn't know each other, but we all thought it was funny, and it didn't bother anybody.

Unknown to us, *Life Magazine* was attending the party to take pictures.

The three of us with the same dress ended up in three separate pictures dancing with beaus or friends, right in the pages of *Life*! What a surprise.

PICTURES TO THE EDITORS
DEBS IN TRIPLICATE

Sirs:

I thought you might be interested in a wartime calamity that turned up at the mass debut at New York's Ritz-Carlton last month (LIFE's Picture of the Week, Jan. 4). The pictures below show three debutantes wearing identical dresses of white starched lace, their swirling skirts scattered with sequins of clover-leaf design.

The girls got together at the party and decided it was a tribute to their mutual good taste.

LOUISE SCHAFFNER
New York, N. Y.

Life At Smith

Life at a women's college in the 1940s did not allow as much freedom from rules as most of us had expected. At Smith, we had to be in our dorm by 10:15 PM, except on Friday and Saturday nights, when midnight was the proverbial witching hour. After curfew the houses were locked, and the housemothers had to personally let any laggards in.

Throughout the war years, most of the service help in the houses had left. We students did all the cleaning, table setting, and waiting for our sit-down dinners.

One of the major distinctives of Smith College was, and still is, "the house system." There was a quadrangle of three and four story dorms with mostly all single-occupancy rooms. Then there were other houses and smaller dorms, ranging in size from ten-beds to over sixty-beds.

During the four years I attended Smith, Waves (Women of the U. S. Navy) took over several campus dorms along with the Hotel Northampton on King Street, built in 1927 and known as "An Inn of Colonial Charm." These Waves were trainees, and they marched around campus looking very spiffy, as if they knew exactly what they were doing.

As part of Hotel Northampton, *Wiggins Tavern* hosted visitors from all over the world. During the war, U.S. Navy Waves billeted at Smith College marched down Main Street three times a day for their meals at Wiggins Tavern. "According to one of them, there were two great things about being stationed in Northampton: 'You survived the war, and you got to eat at Wiggins Tavern'."[1]

"AN INN OF COLONIAL CHARM"

Add from the Smith Alumnae Quarterly, 1946

---

1   http://www.hotelnorthampton.com/history.html

**NEVER BUY RATIONED GOODS
WITHOUT RATION STAMPS**

NEVER PAY MORE THAN THE LEGAL PRICE

United States Office of Price Administration

IMPORTANT: When you have used your ration, salvage the TIN CANS and WASTE FATS. They are needed to make munitions for our fighting men. Cooperate with your local Salvage Committee.

☆ U. S. GOVERNMENT PRINTING OFFICE : 1943   16—35570-1

4

778458 BZ

UNITED STATES OF AMERICA
OFFICE OF PRICE ADMINISTRATION

WAR RATION BOOK FOUR

Issued to _____ Kate H. Belcher _____
(Print first, middle, and last names)

Complete address _____ 430 East 86th St _____

_____ New York _____ N.Y. _____

READ BEFORE SIGNING

In accepting this book, I recognize that it remains the property of the United States Government. I will use it only in the manner and for the purposes authorized by the Office of Price Administration.

Void if Altered _____

(Signature)

It is a criminal offense to violate rationing regulations.

OPA Form R-145   16—35570-1

Smith College had no campus center in those days. But we were allowed, if invited, to eat dinner at other houses. For me, it was a great way to make new friends. My first invitation was quite memorable! Several of my old Brearley classmates had come to Smith with me, and one good friend, Alice, asked me to her house for dinner. I arrived promptly at 5:55, found her room and walked in. Everyone there burst out laughing; I wondered what I had done. Alice introduced me to the group of about eight girls, and more laughter followed. Then she introduced me to another freshman named Louise Burpee. The Belcher-Burpee combo was the cause of all the hilarity. (Louise Burpee, now Louise Landreth, became one of my best friends. To this day, we still talk on the phone from time to time, and get together whenever possible.)

After dinner, we would usually gather for coffee in the living room and chat or play bridge before studying. (Life is so different today. It is only rarely that a whole house eats at the same time—and is there any time for playing bridge?)

Before college, almost all my friends were New Yorkers. Smith has always strived for geographical representation. In my dorm, our class numbered thirty-three. We came from public and private schools all over the USA. During the war years there were not many foreign students, nor many African-Americans, but we were a lively group with varied backgrounds. As I learned more and more about our country, I began to ponder where I might go after graduation. And "where" seemed to be more important to me than "what I would be doing." And so it was to be.

My education at both Brearley and Smith, with their strong female leadership in academic and administrative positions, coupled with the example of my mother and paternal grandmother, all together had developed in me a strong feeling of: "You can do anything if you want it badly enough and work hard enough to get it. It won't be easy, and it won't happen quickly. But keep going."

What I have learned over the years is that this is good advice—even if your goals change, or are changed for you. The effort will be worthwhile.

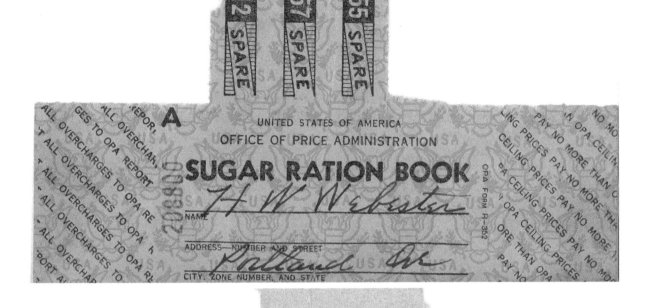

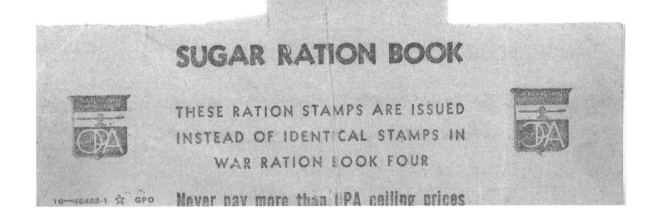

Kate's Presentation, Smith College, "Little Chapel" Service, 16 June 1944

"While reading over some of my favorite poems the other day I suddenly realized that much of my enjoyment came because they effectively carried me out of the present either into a pleasurable anticipation of the future or a happy recollection of the past. It is, I think, too easy for all of us to view the present as a series of complications which loom large as a wave rolling up the beach and breaking. But it is also too easy to forget that troubles too will turn into individual drops and recede in the whole passing scene of life.

"It would do us good, occasionally, to put aside all worries and momentary preoccupations and enjoy the little things in life. By that I mean not only the natural beauty we are exposed to outside but the minute details of daily life which most of us never think about. This need not make us epicureans or even escapists but might help us to live our lives with more consciousness of how full they are, with more realization of the true closeness of God's spirit to us in all we do and all we experience.

"Tonight I'd like to read you two selections: first, a few lines from one of Rupert Brooke's poems to remind you of some of the small, lowly things that we all know; and second, a passage from the 139th Psalm which is a better reminder than any of God's continual presence among us."

"The Great Lover" (Rupert Brooke, 1887–1915, *A treasury Of Great Poems English And American*, by Louis Untermeyer, pp. 1140–1141, 1942.)

These I have loved:
    White plates and cups, clean-gleaming,
Ringed with blue lines; and feathery, faery dust;
Wet roofs, beneath the lamp-light; the strong crust
Of friendly bread; and many-tasting food;
Rainbows; and the blue bitter smoke of wood;
And radiant raindrops couching in cool flowers;
And flowers themselves, that sway through sunny hours,
Dreaming of moths that drink them under the moon…
Hair's fragrance, and the musty reek that lingers
About dead leaves and last year's ferns….

Dear names,
And thousand others throng to me! Royal flames;
Sweet water's dimpling laugh from tap or spring;
Holes in the ground; and voices that do sing:
Voices in laughter, too; and body's pain,
Soon turned to peace; and the deep-panting train;
Firm sands; the little dulling edge of foam
That browns and dwindles as the wave goes home;
And washen stones, gay for an hour; the cold
Graveness of iron; moist black earthen mould;
Sleep; and high places; footprints in the dew;
And oaks; and brown horse-chestnuts, glossy-new;
And new-peeled sticks; and shining pools on grass;—
All these have been my loves.

Psalm 139 (New International Version, ©2011)
 1 You have searched me, LORD,
  and you know me.
2 You know when I sit and when I rise;
  you perceive my thoughts from afar.
3 You discern my going out and my lying down;
  you are familiar with all my ways.
4 Before a word is on my tongue
  you, LORD, know it completely.
5 You hem me in behind and before,
  and you lay your hand upon me.
6 Such knowledge is too wonderful for me,
  too lofty for me to attain.

Lead Article: "Campus Vibrates to First Peacetime Commencement" (by Dorothy Hamilton Dick)

SMITH
ALUMNAE QUARTERLY
AUGUST 1946

Graduation "Ivy Procession." Kate is in the fourth row back. Photograph by Fred G. Chase.

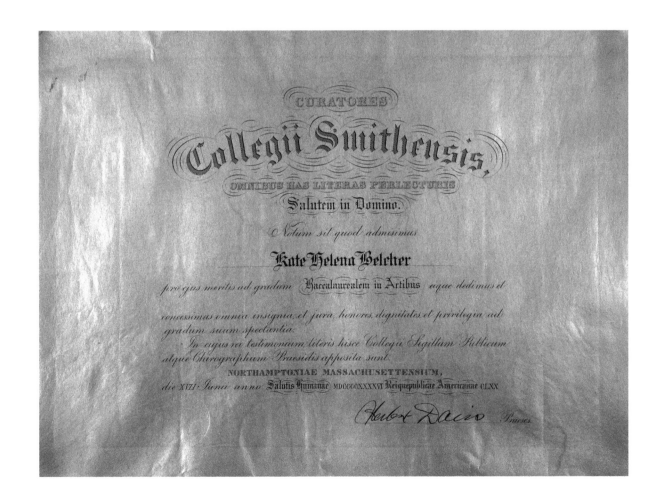

Barbara O'Brien

Going through old
pix for various
reasons & finally
found this gem —
it should get you
some respect!
The "wow" was
written in 1941
or whenever.

♡

Part II

Washington Stories

Smith Tower, Seattle, WA[1]

Heading West

June 1946. Graduation.

As I left Smith, I knew that my family, my friends, my education, all added up to an extraordinary foundation for moving on in life, on my own. I had had more than a fair share of love and care.

Goodbyes said, I traveled across the country for the first time to visit friends. Travels took me to Louisville, Kentucky, Cleveland, Ohio, then Chicago, San Francisco, and finally Portland, Oregon, for the wedding of my cousin "Chil" Ashmun and my former roommate Candy McKee.

---

1 Photographer: C.F. Todd ,Sepia, 1917. University of Washington Libraries Digital Collections (http:// content.lib.washington.edu/). Public Domain. Source: image https://commons.wikimedia.org/wiki/ File:Pioneer_square.jpg

All of July and August was spent visiting friends, being royally entertained. I meet all kinds of people and realized that New York City was not the only wonderful place in the world.

September 4th of 1946, Portland. I was to be in the wedding of Chil and Candy. I enjoyed three weeks of new experiences, discovering high mountains and beautiful lakes, and being spoiled by many McKee friends. Several of our classmates joined our group. Mrs. McKee was amazing! She seemed to take it all in stride, though I suspect she must have been delighted when the mob left.

The wedding was a big one, with eight bridesmaids and eight ushers. Early on I had asked Candy who all the ushers were. She named seven of them and I said, "Well, who's the eighth?" She said, "Oh, he's Holt Webster—a bit older than the others, and not your type." I learned that Holt was working in Seattle and would only be around for the weekend before the wedding. When I met him, he was amusing, easy to talk to, and a great "tease." He did not seem "old" to me!

The wedding reception was at the McKee home, and during the festivities I discovered that my sister Suzie and I both thought we had a late date with the same boy. She liked him better than I did, so I "developed" a bad headache and was about to climb the stairs to bed when the front door opened and Holt Webster walked in. I ran up to him and said, "Oh, there you are. I've been looking for you." It was a big lie, but I didn't want to leave the party and he was available. We had a great time and ended up talking, after everyone else disappeared, until 3:00 AM.

Holt went back to Seattle the next day, but not before we made a date for the one night that part of the family and I were going to spend at Seattle's Olympic Hotel.

Aunt Mary, Johnny Ashmun, Russ Belcher, Gayle Young, and I took the train the following day to Seattle. I will never forget the taxi ride from the King Street Station to the "Olympic." I looked out the back window as we were about on Third and Marion Street and thought we would roll back down to the bay. It was so steep!

Holt joined us—at Aunt Mary's insistence—for dinner in the Georgian Room, and then we walked to what Holt called his "Club." It was on Pike Street and Boren, a Veteran's Club. He had a locker with a bottle (bourbon in those days), and there was music and dancing. We danced and talked for hours and then walked along wooden sidewalks back to the hotel. That was our first date and, I was amazed, the next date was not until January, four months later.

The next day, we, the family, started on our trip through the Canadian Rockies to a ranch named "Skookumchuck" in British Columbia; it was owned by an old school friend of Aunt Mary's. That week was really the beginning of the rest of my life, although I wasn't at all aware of it at the time.

Aunt Mary, my three boy cousins and I had a fabulous trip through Banff, Lake Louise, and then driving over the mountains to the ranch.

One small incident. During this trip, we got a flat tire on a lonely mountain road. We were driving a rental car, and the spare tire was also flat. Cousin Russ Belcher was prone to asthma attacks, so we decided he should hitch a ride and take the flat tire back to town. It was a hot and dusty, treeless spot. Soon someone drove by in a pickup truck and Cousin Russ took off. The remaining four of us remained with the car. Aunt Mary had a bottle of bourbon, some chocolate bars, and a pack of cards. So, the four of us sat in the disabled, hot car and played bridge, drank, and nibbled melting chocolate for some two hours until Russ returned, after which we were on our way.

We had a wonderful few days with lots of marvelous scenery there at that ranch in the mountains; then on to Calgary, then flew home from there.

Back in New York City, I announced to Mother and Dad that I had decided to go to San Francisco to get a job and learn about life on the West Coast. They both took it in stride. Their only request was that I had to have a place to live before leaving New York City. Somehow I thought it would all happen—eternally the optimist. And it did!

A week later, I was at a party and talking with an old friend who had just graduated from Vassar. She mentioned that her ex-roommate was in Berkeley, California, and was looking for someone to share a rental.

So in early December 1946, I flew to San Francisco. I was met by my newest friend, Lydia Brewster, and subsequently settled into the bottom floor of a rental house in the hills of Berkeley. I rode the tram (there was no BART in those days) looking for work and soon found a job at Crown-Zellerbach, a large paper company, in their training program. They set me to organizing shelves of paper files in a huge room; amazingly, I really enjoyed the challenge. (I still like to set up files.)

We had time to wander around Berkeley, San Francisco, and the whole Bay Area, which was a great way to experience post-war America. I never found out where the training program was leading, because after four months—and six dates with Holt Webster—we became engaged.

When we called Mom and Dad to tell them the news of my engagement, they were amazing. They were very calm and kind and welcoming to Holt, no questions asked. That surprised me, because they had not yet even met him. Although I had written about Holt, I had expected a least some reservations and some suggestions that we were rushing too fast. When I asked about their reaction some time later, Mom simply said, "You had spent your life asking questions about whether to do this or that. This time you were positive and had no questions." She added, "Your father and I quickly decided you had grown up and knew what you wanted, and we trusted you."

A New York City Wedding

Crown-Zellerbach graciously accepted my two-week resignation notice. I flew back to New York City to prepare for our wedding. On May 27, 1947, I became Mrs. Holt W. Webster. We were married in Epiphany Church in the city, by the Reverend Charles Gompf, Rector of Grace Episcopal Church, Newark, New Jersey. He had married Mother and Dad and had baptized me.

The wedding and reception were large and lovely, mostly Mother and Dad's friends and a few "Smithies." While we were receiving the guests, Holt asked if everyone in New York City was a physician—it did seem that way to both of us.

After a three day honeymoon in the Pocono Mountains, we flew to Seattle to settle into our small rental home. It was the first floor of an old house on Capitol Hill on 15th Avenue East,

across from Volunteer Park. We had a living room, dining room and kitchen, including steps to a small backyard. We shared an upstairs bath with two other couples, each of whom had just a bedroom. The bathtub was almost seven feet long. One of the couples, who were artists, had painted a huge mural of two reclining nudes on the wall over the tub. The painting was tastefully done, but it always a shock to our guests—especially to my mother!

Our only Seattle connection was Holt's first cousin, Craig Wallace and his wife Polly. They lived nearby and had three young children. Through them, and people whom Holt met at work (Northwest Airlines), and the Smith College Club, we made friends. I've always thought, however, that since we did not really know each other very well, having no family or "close old ties" was fortuitous. We really had time to get to know each other, to give and take and talk things out without having to explain our "goings on" to anyone else. It was a great start to a close and lasting marriage.

Holt wanted to leave Portland, along with all his family and connections, to start life fresh.

Newton Street Years

Two weeks after our first child, Kelly, was born on June 24, 1948, we moved into our first house, just a few blocks away on Capitol Hill. We never guessed that this Newton Street Neighborhood would be our home for twenty-five years.

The first few years of marriage were a learning process for all the years to come: how to communicate, compromise, support, and enjoy life with my chosen partner; how to cope with three children, born within four years of each other; and, of course, learning how to manage a house and make it into a home for us all.

Right before Craig was born, Kelly was very excited about having a new baby in the house. In those days we still had no idea what sex a baby was going to be, and it didn't matter to us. Craig was born on June 16, 1950. Kelly was just two, and she took it upon herself to take care of him. He was a healthy and easy baby, sleeping, eating, and laughing a lot. So, the first couple years of his life, his big sister took good care of him. As a result, he was a lazy lump and very chubby.

Craig was almost fifteen months old, a pudgy little boy, before he got up and started to walk. Though once he started walking, he lost weight quickly and seemed to be always on the run the rest of his life. He didn't talk much either, until nearly the end of his first year. He didn't need to, because Kelly knew everything he wanted. She provided him with toys, she played with him, and talked steadily to him. At the time, I didn't realize how much effect it had on Craig. But he felt very loved and cared for, and Kelly certainly made things easier for her mom in those days.

When Kelly was two and a half years and Craig six months old, "BA" (before Annie), Holt decided it was time to leave Northwest Airlines. He wanted to start an airfreight business with an older colleague, Phil Gruger. Phil had worked in various areas of the airline industry and felt that the time for growth in airfreight had arrived. Phil was a dreamer and an optimist, while Holt was a pragmatic planner who always looked out for possible problems. They made a great team, and with a secretary to run the office, they started Pacific Air Freight in January 1951.

The office was a small two room area on Marion Street just west of Western Avenue. That was the beginning, and we certainly never imagined what the future would be, and how it would change our lives.

It was at this point that I began to see a new Holt evolving. He knew that PAF was going to take all his concentration and energy. It was likewise probable that, financially, it would be a long haul before we saw steady success. Holt's approach to this challenge was to call for what would be the first of an ongoing series of family planning sessions.

"Your job, Kate," Holt said, "is to raise the children, run the house, pay the bills, plan our social life, and keep me posted on all of that."

I remember saying, "Is that all?"

Actually my "job" put structure into my life and gave me an opportunity to plan and set goals, and, I had to admit, being in charge was a challenge I looked forward to.

In order to develop the company, Holt began to travel. PAF started by delivering flowers to Alaska, and then new products up and down the West Coast. Before long, he was checking into large urban areas all across the United States. Holt wanted the children to understand (as best they could) what he was doing; Kelly remembers Saturday mornings sorting out invoices of different colors.

Our house on Newton Street was on a corner at the top of a hill, right up next to our neighbors Hod and Anne White's house. In fact we were only six feet away. Our back door, the one we used most often, was practically up against their house. Every morning, for years, Holt would leave for work by 7:00 AM. He would call up to the window by the back door, "Time to get up! Beth, it's morning!" Across that short distance to the White's house was Beth's room. We could hear the groans, but it became a ritual they could count on, and they never were late for school.

Another tradition on Newton Street, that apparently went with our house—so we were told by Hod White—revolved around the first snowfall of winter. It was in the early fifties, and the first big snowfall of our first winter there, that Hod explained: "It is a tradition, when the snow becomes deep enough, that the people who live in this house have a hot chocolate and cookie party, and then we all go sledding." Our house was at the top of the hill. So, we blocked off the street all the way down the hill to East Boston Street, and then everybody went sledding. We followed this tradition through most of the 1950s. Fortunately no one ever got hurt. It was great fun, typical of the time. (Imagine, today, a bunch of dads getting away with blocking off a major street for a sled party!)

One other Newton Street tradition, which was my idea, was met with mixed feelings on the part of my children. The first few years we had wonderful family Christmases. But we were alone with no family around, and I missed our Christmas holidays with all my extended family in New York or Far Hills.

Therefore, after the first couple of quiet family Christmases, I felt we needed to share with others around us. Holt and I decided to have an eggnog party for our Newton Street neighbors on Christmas afternoon. It would be an open house from 2:00 to 5:00 for the whole neighborhood, not all of whom we knew at that time. We sent the word up and down the street.

We held this afternoon Christmas open house for years, until we moved to Bainbridge Island in the early 1970s.

The problem the children had was that they had to clean up their new toys and other presents in the living room before 2:00 PM, and make everything clean and tidy. But they were always good sports and very helpful. We had cookies and eggnog and fruit punch. It was amazing how many neighbors would turn up. We made many good friends up and down both sides of the street. Eventually, other friends, who might be feeling a little bit lonely, also would show up. I have always appreciated that my family joined with me to host this Christmas afternoon open house.

Life on Newton Street was fairly routine. In the 1950s, daycare nurseries and preschools had not yet become an accepted part of our community, but the post-war baby crop was booming at record pace.

Many of my friends had their own growing families, and before long we had developed a wonderful system of morning coffee hour. Two or three times a week, each mom would bundle up the youngsters—we had no car seats then—and drive off to different homes. We took turns hosting the morning coffee gatherings, and we all enjoyed a couple hours of chatting amidst the noise and confusion of babies and toddlers.

Capitol Hill, Washington Park, and Laurelhurst were where most of us lived, so distances were not great. We did have a few friends across the lake, but in those days that drive seemed much too far.

When Kelly was six, she experienced one of the early disappointments of her life. My sister Suzie asked Kelly to be a flower-girl in her wedding to Ed Platt. The celebration was set to be in Midland, Texas, in June. We found a lovely little long yellow dress, and Kelly was very excited about it. The week before Holt, Kelly and I were preparing to go to Midland, Kelly came down with a very severe case of measles. And that was that, she couldn't go. She was so disappointed.

We kept the dress for years and years.

She tried it on a few times, before she outgrew it.

Around the same time Kelly began to draw and paint. She loved to draw things! I began to realized Kelly had real artistic talent, an ability no one in the Belcher family had at all (we were musical, but not visual artists). But the Websters, both Holt's mother and father, were artistic, both drew and painted.

Kelly kept on drawing and painting all through elementary school, and on through college. To this day, her pictures are scattered all through our house. One of my very favorite pictures of hers is one she painted, when she was twelve years old, of our Newton Street house.

Kelly was always the one to make place cards, decorate Christmas cards, and do all those fun touches that her mother was not capable of even thinking about doing.

Perhaps my most favorite work of art which Kelly made for us appears every Christmas when I unpack the decorations. It is a mosaic,

Before remodeling, *steep stairs led down from a boxy front porch to the sloping street*

DON NORMARK
Elevated walkway *pulls house entrance closer to crest of hill. Shingled fence off side of house provides privacy for dining room behind*

Old tight approach becomes generous

Christmas figures done on little circles of cardboard with carefully cut out pieces of gold, silver and blue paper depicting Madonna, Baby Jesus, and others figures. The work is utterly amazing! Especially that she was only twelve at the time.

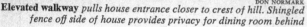

On the weeks that Holt was not traveling for PAF, we always had dinner together in the dining room with a fairly formal setting. The idea was to teach the children how to have dinner with the Queen, if the time should ever come, or at least to learn some manners. We had lots of discussions about proper dinner conversation and etiquette, and once a year we even brought out our wedding present finger bowls so they would know how to cope with that experience.

One evening, when Kelly was about thirteen, Craig eleven, and Annie nine, we were all sitting together around the table, and Holt was lecturing the children as he often did. Clearly, he didn't think he was lecturing, or intending to sound like that, it was just the tone of his voice and his way of speaking when he was telling the children something. In the middle of a sentence, suddenly all three children raised their hands. Holt looked at me to see if I knew what it was all about. I shrugged my shoulders—I didn't know what they were up to.

Holt said to the children, "Would you all like to be excused?"

Kelly, who was generally the spokesperson for the kids, said, "No, Dad. We have all decided that from time to time you really do pontificate, and you go on and on talking about something that you want us to know and understand. And we usually get it long before you think we do. So, from now on, when we have gotten the point, we will raise our hands."

Holt sat there for a moment, then burst out laughing! And that was the end of it.

However, none of the Webster family have ever forgotten that evening. And on varying occasions—even though Holt is no longer with us—hands go up, and we'll look at each other and get the point immediately.

Our Big City Seattle Children

Holt continued building Pacific Air Freight. It was an enormous commitment, but an exciting and unpredictable adventure.

The next four years were busy. Anne McCraken joined her siblings on March 17, 1952. I was a stay-at-home mom and maid of all things domestic.

Holt worked long hours, six days a week. I kept the house running smoothly, kept the children in good health, and managed the finances. It was a challenge, particularly the last part, but I worked through it and enjoyed this new life.

In 1952, we moved up the street to a larger house. There were more children in the new part of the neighborhood, on both sides of Newton Street. Two generations of our neighbors have become life-long friends of all the Websters. We could not have found a better environment for raising our family.

That summer of 1952, our friends John and Ann Powel invited us to a picnic on Bainbridge Island, west of Seattle across Puget Sound. They had just bought some property for a summer place and wanted us to buy part of it and be neighbors. We loved the idea but had no money, having just used it all on a down-payment for our Newton Street home. Johnny Powel offered to wait for reimbursement. We were thrilled, if a little scared, to have a summer place. What wonderful friends the Powels were (and still are). Johnny and Ann made it possible for us to have the best of all worlds.

I almost managed to cancel the whole "deal" by accidentally slamming our car door on four-year-old "Babe" Powel's fingers as we were leaving the property. We all rushed down to the one island physician for help; there was no permanent damage, and we could all smile with relief.

We called our new Bainbridge Island summer cottage, the Little Red House. I painted it, with Muffy Williams' help, in 1953. We had bought it in 1952.

The funny story, we had to paint it right away in order to preserve it. I wanted it barn red. However, the base coat was bright pink. People stopped by and said, "Is that the color of your house?" I explained, "It's going to be barn red."

We enjoyed that cottage Easter to Thanksgiving, and all summer long.

We also built a tennis court. Our neighbors, the Powels, had a saltwater swimming pool, which completed our summer resort, entertaining the next generation for many years.

End of 1971 we tore down the Little Red House, having enjoyed our last Thanksgiving there. We came back the following week to clear everything out before it was to be demolished. As we rounded the corner we heard a great noise. The bulldozers had already started demolition!

I burst into tears at the unexpected sight. Our neighbor Jeff Powel came walking up to our car. He said in his kindly voice, "Don't cry. I have this. Here," and he handed me the bathtub stopper dangling on a long chain. The last artifact rescued.

I grabbed the drain stopper and felt a little better. We had that tub stopper gilded in gold and it has hung on our Christmas tree ever since.

We hold dear memories of the Little Red House and the many summers we enjoyed there.

The first big event in our new Sunnybranch home was on December 27th 1972, a party for Mother and Dad, the "Doctors Belcher," for their 50th wedding anniversary. It was a happy occasion for the whole family!

On reaching school age, still living in Seattle, our children all walked the few blocks down the hill with neighbors to Seward Public Elementary School on Roanoke Street and Franklin Avenue. (Today the school is on the other side of the Freeway.)

Each of the children did well at school until Craig entered the third grade and had a very hard time learning to read. I spoke about this with his teacher and then with the principal of the school, who was reputed to be an expert in reading. She said, "He'll be just fine. He'll be reading by the end of third grade." I thought: well, that's great; but if he is still having trouble reading, what do we do then? So I did some research and found a tutoring service in the University District, which

worked with elementary school age children in remedial reading. They tested Craig and found out that his problem was not phonetics generally, but was a problem with comprehension of ver-

bal particles, the small connecting words such as "but," "this," "and." I enrolled him in their course.

From January to May of Craig's third grade year, Monday, Wednesday, and Friday, I drove Craig to the University District—maybe a fifteen minute drive during rush hour, five o'clock every day—and then picked him up at seven o'clock.

And it worked! We were so grateful, at the end of that time, that we had stuck it out. It had played havoc with our dinner hour, and other activities, but it was well worth it.

Kelly left Seward and went to St. Nicholas in the sixth grade. She was unhappy at first because she had been appointed "chief patrol officer" for her next year at Seward, but it was time for a change. Two of her Newton Street pals also were going, and that made walking to school more palatable.

Kelly was a conscientious student, made friends easily, and handled responsibility well. During her second year she began complaining about one of her teachers; Kelly said this teacher was unfair, picked on students for no apparent reason, and was inconsistent in her demands. I suggested to Kelly that perhaps she was being overly sensitive, and that, in the future, she would be called upon to work with all kinds of people. "Try harder to understand your teacher's requirements." But two weeks later that teacher was removed from her job—she had had a nervous breakdown. I apologized to Kelly and vowed that, in the future, we would discuss situations more fully, from both sides.

From the time she was eleven or twelve, Kelly's favorite occupation was baby-sitting. We had several families on Newton Street with young children. They all loved Kelly, and she kept very busy. Kelly has always has been a creative thinker; that, coupled with her artistic abilities and her fertile imagination, has served her well—and still does.

In 1954, Mary Fite Black asked if we would be interested in joining a group of families, six or eight, planning to buy a ski cabin in Snoqualmie, which was owned by her family. It sounded like fun to us, so we said, "Yes!" The cabin was situated near the edge of the main ski slope to the right of the number one T-bar. It was a large log cabin with a big downstairs, fireplace, cook stove, benches and tables, and two lofts in the upper A-frame. The first loft had three single-level bunks, while the second loft was divided into two more private sections. The loft ladder was a challenge at night. There was no indoor plumbing; an outhouse stood across a small creek some twenty-five feet from the cabin.

Several families often gathered at the cabin on weekends. It was a wonderful getaway! The Powels and other friends used it until it was donated to the Boy Scouts in the early 1960s. Later it was sold and taken down. Snoqualmie Ski Resort has expanded across the area where it once stood.

As the children got to be around five, seven, and nine, we decided to send them up on the ski bus every Saturday to Snoqualmie Falls. Holt worked on Saturdays, and though he did like to ski, he explained that he was not expendable at the office and he could not take the chance of breaking a leg or being out of work as he recovered from some skiing accident.

About a month after they started their weekend ski trips, they came to me one Saturday afternoon. Kelly, always the spokesperson, said, "Mom, we don't want to ride the ski bus anymore. It's diesel, it smells. We have to eat our sandwiches on the bus, and it's just awful. Besides, we don't know anybody else that rides the bus." She caught her breath, then continued. "Mom, you like to exercise. You really need to learn to ski. So we think you should take us up there every Saturday."

So I did. For several years, I learned to ski along with my three children. I was never as skilled as they were, but I really did love it.

Vern Williams used to take his children up skiing on Saturdays, also. He was a much better skier than I. After about a year of all of us skiing together, he told me, "Kate, it is time for you to get off the T-bar and onto the chair-lift." I shook my head, saying, "I don't like heights; the chair-lift scares me." He laughed, "Nothing ever happens on a chair-lift. Come on. You can do it. Let's go." So he got me on the chair, and we started up the hill. About a half a minute later, someone three chairs ahead of me fell off his chair.

We weren't very high up yet, and the snow was quite deep, so the person didn't get hurt. But I was terrified! When we reached the top, I didn't think I could get off. Thanks to Vern, I managed without even falling down. It was the only time I ever saw that happen. Nonetheless, I never really enjoyed getting off a chair. But skiing down the hill was well worth the challenge.

At the time Craig was finishing sixth grade at Seward, we hoped that he would be able to go to Lakeside School. But he didn't make the cut that year, so he attended Meany Middle School, on 21st Street, not too far from our house.

The first day Craig went to school riding his bike and came home walking it. His bike had been stripped sometime during the school day. So from then on he either walked or I drove him to school every day.

He did quite well. He was small for his age, and he wasn't a fighter. He survived, but it was a difficult year for him.

At the end of that year, we decided it would be good for Craig to go to boarding school. We toured some prep schools on the East Coast. At that point, I called Lakeside School and asked if Craig could take the PSAT test for application to independent schools. He took the PSAT, and two weeks later the admissions director, Bob Spock, called me and said, "Your son has really grown up this year. We would like him to come to Lakeside." It was a wonderful surprise! We really didn't want him to go to boarding school, so everyone was happy about that. Craig was enrolled and stayed there until he graduated.

One of Craig's experiences, that neither Holt nor I will ever forget, happened one night of his sophomore year at Lakeside. We had been out to dinner, and came home perhaps a little earlier than planned, 10:30 or so. The light was on in

the livingroom. Craig was sitting all cuddled up in the corner of the sofa looking rather bleary. It took only a minute talking to him to realize he'd been drinking. We asked him, "What have *you* been doing?" He replied, "Well, you always told me if I was going to drink I should drink at home. I was testing your advice." I asked, "What were you drinking, Craig?" "Bourbon and Coke," he admitted, which was about the worst combination we could imagine. Holt and I just burst out laughing, and then sent him up to bed. It was a lesson for us all and made it easier to talk about other teen-age escapades.

When he was twelve or thirteen, Craig announced he was going to be an architect. He never lost this aspiration.

One unforgettable junior year incident at Lakeside concerned Craig's difficulty with basic physics. I spoke with his teacher and asked, "How will he be able to be an architect?" The teacher replied, "By the time he gets into that profession, it will all be done on computers!"

Lakeside was a good experience for Craig. He made quite a few friends, did well, and upon graduation went to Colgate College.

Annie attended Seward, with Kelly and Craig. She was a model child, quiet. She watched her brother and sister, and the sometimes naughty things they did, and seemed to learn from them what not to do—or at least how not to get caught.

Years later I asked her about that and she said, "Well, I just always figured out what they had done, and then I could do something different, and you'd probably never know."

Therefore it was surprising to Holt and me, when in the fifth grade Annie started being naughty. It was very much out of character for her. She would do just little things, nothing destructive. But there was a distinct difference in her whole attitude. After a couple weeks watching this change, I decided she was just bored and not being challenged at school.

A visit to Seward and talks with her teacher and the principal, to suggest a little extra work or some reading assignments or a project of some kind, bore little fruit. Their reply: "No, we can't do that, it's not possible." So, we decided it was time to find some other way for her to be challenged. Fortunately, the fifth grade at St. Nicholas had space for another student. After Christmas break that year, Annie started at St. Nicholas, and was back to being a model child again—at least as far as I knew.

Annie's years at St. Nicholas were fairly quiet. She made a few very close friends and continued to be involved in school activities.

From the time she was eight years old, her greatest joy has been riding. On Bainbridge Island, we had at first a pony then a horse. Neither were spectacular animals, but Annie loved them.

In the winters, two or three afternoons a week, Annie and I would drive across Lake Washington to barns in Bellevue or Issaquah where she would go riding. Driving over at 4:00 PM wasn't so bad; but returning home during rush-hour via the I-90 floating bridge, the only bridge in those days, could be very trying—particularly in winter when it was cold and raining and often icy.

Annie also took riding lessons in the summers with a wonderful woman named Barbara Wilkinson. Often, as well, she would ride around the east side of Bainbridge Island with her friend Babe Powel, who also had her own horse.

One day in August, I dropped Annie off for her lesson with Barbara, then went to the only grocery store on the island at that time, Town & Country. Mother and Dad were arriving the next day for their annual August visit. I had just filled one shopping basket, and was about to start a second load, when Barbara rushed into the store and said, "You need to come right away. Annie fell, and the horse kicked her, and she's in the doctor's office across the street." I told the Town & Country people I'd be back as soon as possible for the food.

We rushed across the street to Dr. Sinclair Walts' office. Annie was being held down by the nurse who said, "Can you hold her still; the doctor needs to stitch her up." "Of course," I said. (This conversation is certainly not one you would hear today in a doctor's office or emergency room.) I held her and could see the bone of her scalp exposed, she'd been kicked in the back of the head. She was stitched up, and for two or three days, she was drowsy. But she recovered and was back on the horse sooner than we expected.

A year or so later, Annie and Babe Powel were riding back from a horse show in Winslow. Holt and I drove down the highway to see where they were and spotted a crowd on the road and a pony standing quietly. Annie had fallen off from exhaustion and was sound asleep lying there on the ground. Holt had to ride the pony home.

Often it seems that the remembrance of events we retain most vividly of our children are when they get sick or injured!

1967. Craig was sixteen when he asked if he could drive up to Crystal Mountain so he and Annie could go skiing, just the two of them. With some trepidation, Holt and I decided it had to happen soon or later, so we agreed. Craig and Annie took off in our Ford station wagon.

As it happened, I had a friend visiting from the East Coast, who wanted a tour of Seattle. So, we picked her up, toured Seattle together, had lunch, then put her on the train and went home. As we pulled up to the house, Hod White, our neighbor, ran up and announced, "Craig called about half an hour ago and said he was bringing Annie down from the mountain; she had been hit by another skier. They should arrive in a few minutes."

Craig drove up and rushed from the car to meet us, telling us about Annie's accident.

In those days, we always kept a sleeping bag in the back of the station wagon just in case something happened, and Annie was wrapped up in it in the back seat. I opened the back door, Annie took one look at me, leaned over and threw up.

Craig said, "She didn't do that before!"

We asked what had happened.

Craig explained that they'd been skiing down Green River Valley slope. Annie had fallen in a turn, and some man came barreling down behind her and ran into her as she was trying to get up. The man didn't stop, just continued on down the hill. Craig said, "I looked for a second, Mom, and wondered whether to go chase him or see about Annie; I decided to stay with Annie."

We were very grateful Craig had made the right decision.

Craig then called for help, and the ski patrol came and towed her down to the lodge. They put out a call for any available doctors, and two doctors skied over. It just happened that they were both our doctors, Dr. Jack Docter, medical director at Children's Hospital, and Dr. Barrett, who was our family physician. Craig told us that they took one look at Annie and said, "She has a concussion; get her down to Swedish Hospital."

When I heard what they had told Craig, I asked, "Dr. Docter said take her to Swedish?"

Craig said, "Well, Dr. Barrett said that, and Dr. Docter didn't want to contradict him."

"Well," I responded, "I'll contradict him. Let's go right now to Children's."

I was on the board of Children's and I had called ahead, asking who was on duty. I knew the physician on call for that weekend, and he said, "I'll meet you at the door."

Annie was released after three days. The only repercussions, were that once in a while she had a little trouble with hyperventilation, if she got too excited or upset. And we soon had that under control. We all survived.

Holt and I were very proud of sixteen year old Craig in the way he had handled the situation.

Upon graduating from Colgate University, Craig took a year off, joining us on our Europe trip. He then went to the University of Wisconsin in Milwaukee where he obtained a masters in architecture, after which he joined Bassetti Architects, who designed the 37-story Henry M. Jackson

Federal Building in Seattle in 1974. Craig then went into business for himself as C.L. Webster Architects, certified with the AIA (American Institute of Architects).

Among the houses Craig designed is his sister Annie Fox's home on Mercer Island. He also designed affordable, subsidized housing on Lopez Island—a tradition carried on by his company to the present day, including projects across Washington State in communities such as Clarkston, Orcas and Lummi islands.

Sevil Gence

The summer of 1965. Kelly was about to enter her senior year at St. Nicholas.

We had signed up and were looking forward to a foreign student, through AFS Intercultural Programs, whom we had learned was arriving from Turkey. I knew little about Turkey at the time, and my limited understanding was rather old-fashioned. I expected her to be shy and unsophisticated.

In June, Sevil Gence arrived on a bus, and we were there to meet her. She was a year younger than Kelly, petite, dark, pretty, and very lively—full of bounce and smiles. She spoke superb English. Her family lived in Ankara. Her father was an import-exporter. With two brothers and a sister, she was the youngest of four. Her oldest brother was the leader of the most famous Jazz band in Turkey at that time.

We drove to Bainbridge Island where we were already ensconced for the summer. That first evening was very chatty; Sevil never stopped talking. "Sev," as we all came to call her, went to bed in the bunkhouse with Kelly and Annie. Craig was on the other side. Sev slept later in the morning than my children, who were up, dressed, and having breakfast by the time she turned up. (I thought it was jet-lag, but as it turned out it was Sev; she always slept late, and she's still doing it, as far as I know.)

That first morning, the conversation went as follows. I asked, "What would you like for breakfast?" Sev replied, "What did your children have?" "Scrambled eggs, bacon, toast, and orange juice." "Well," she said, "I would like that, too." "But, Sev, you aren't supposed to eat bacon, your religion says that is forbidden." Sev looked at me and said, "Mom—" she had immediately started calling me Mom "—Mom, that's old fashioned. Mohammed said you couldn't have pork of any kind because they were dirty animals. Today, everything is all cleaned up and sanitary, and of course I'll eat bacon."

Sev stayed with us for a whole year and became an integral part of our family.

We still keep in touch, to this day. She had gone back to Turkey and after three months told her father she just could not be a Turkish woman anymore. She wanted to go to London and study design. She still lives in London, having developed a very successful office design company. She works all over Europe and is very highly regarded professionally. She has had a wonderful life. It's fun to keep up with her. We all see her every time we travel to London and it was a special treat to have her back on Bainbridge Island recently for Kelly's 60th birthday.

My First Time Abroad!

I was 44 years old, before I made my first trip abroad. Being brought up during the Depression years, and then the war years, had made travel impossible, and, as I had gotten married right after the war and started raising a family, there was no time or money for travel then either.

In 1968, Kelly was in Paris for her junior year abroad and had some vacation time. She and I spent two or three days in Paris. Then we met up with an English friend, Jackie, who had lived on Newton Street for years. She had moved back to England and was in the travel business there. I had written to ask if she would like to drive Kelly and me around the UK for a couple weeks—and I'd pay all expenses. Jackie replied back that she would be delighted.

We stayed in bed-and-breakfasts from London, all the way up the East Coast as far as Troon Scotland. Then we traveled to Aberdeen, back through Edinburgh, then south to York, and back down to London.

What a fascinating trip!

Kelly's recollection is that Jackie never stopped talking, which was true. She was amusing and full of fascinating information—which we decided to believe, because we had no reason not to.

I went back to Paris with Kelly to help her settle in for the fall. While we were there she was worried that it was going to be a cold winter, and she would want a hot water bottle. "Madame," she explained, "just doesn't have enough blankets for my roommate and me." They were staying with a retired widow.

So, we went to the drugstore. Kelly couldn't think of the French name for "hot water bottle." So I said to the druggist, in my halting French, "I need something to keep me warm when I sleep." He burst out laughing! And I realized then what I had said. After a minute he did find a hot water bottle.

We had a grand holiday!

Dear Daddy and Craigy and Annie,

Here we are in England,
That lovely Isle,
Where people speak strangely
And rarely ever smile.

The weather's been typical
Seattle—like rain.
And cheery old Mom says,
"We'll come again!"

In our cute Cortina
We've been far and near;
J and K in the front seat
And me in the rear (with the purses and the food and the
            mackintoshes and mom's suitcases!)

We've seen most of England
I could tell you a lot
Except that I'm sleepy
And I've mostly forgot.

It's green in the south part
Roads winding around
Rivers. And all of this country
Is dotted with towns. (What began as a poetic device turned into
            fiasco. Please use imagination with this verse.)
The middle of England
Is industrial waste
We sped by on the motorway
At a rather fast pace.
The northland is rocky.

Rock fences and sheep
Cover the countryside.
It gets rather steep.

Suzanne Pettit & Kelly In Paris

Mrs. Cave Bigley
Talks quite a bit
And mom is her listener
And I mostly sit.

But I'm having a ball
And "doing it right."
That's about the extent
I can get out tonight.

'Cept we sleep with hot water bottles
And get tea when we wake
Which is not as good as at four
When we get tea and cake!

Well sweet 'os I miss you
And wish I were there.
'Cept I'm loving each minute
With dear old ma here.

Love, Kelly
(Probably such verse as this was never composed
as on this day of our Lord 12 September 1968)

Julia Child Comes To Dinner

The year was 1973. We had been living in our new house on Bainbridge Island for just a few months when a friend from St. Mark's Cathedral, Seattle, called and said, "Kate, Julia Child is coming to Seattle to do a money-raiser for the Cathedral. She has asked that she be entertained for the three nights before her program in various homes in the area, and that each of them would be unique, with different foods, ambiance, families. Therefore, we thought of you and how it would be wonderful if she came to Bainbridge Island, to your house for dinner."

I was a little startled by the idea. But I was also thrilled at the thought and said, "Of course. We would be delighted to do that."

Julia was scheduled to come to Seattle the end of March.

Holt Webster always said that the six weeks before Julia Child came to dinner were the most difficult six weeks of his life, because I was stewing the whole time about what I was going to feed her, and how it was all going to work out. In that respect, it was a tough time for me, too.

The plan was that she would come with her entourage, which consisted of her husband Paul and two of her assistants who traveled with her to help with her programs. There would also be two or three people, whom I knew, joining us from the Cathedral. I could also invite a few neighbors and friends.

We ended up deciding upon eighteen for dinner. Twelve could fit comfortably around our large dining room table, and just outside the dining room we had a table that seated six. Even with the two separate tables, the seating was intimate and made for easy conversing among all of us—one big happy party!

Eventually I decided that what I would do was a local Northwest dinner, because that would allow me to prepare a menu that would be very different from anything Julia did, and I wouldn't feel I had to compete with her cooking talents. Bainbridge Island was a place where native seafood and produce contributed to a unique local cuisine.

We started with a clam broth. I went to my neighbor's and dug up two pails of small, and slightly illegal, clams. I steamed them in chicken broth with a little white wine and some garlic. The broth was served in bouillon cups with a few tiny clams floating on top. At this point, as the evening was just getting going, Julia turned to Holt and asked the name of the wine being served.

Holt smiled and answered, "Well, Julia, it's white wine"—he never did remember the names of any wine.

From there, we progressed to the entrée, which was one whole Dungeness crab for each person. The crabs came from Pike Place Market; after I explained what was going on, they cleaned them for me. I asked, "But how do I prepare them?" They explained, "We clean and pre-cook them. Here's what you do: in the stomachs you put a tablespoon of butter and some herbs, and then wrap each whole individual crab in foil and put them in the oven at 425 degrees for about fifteen to twenty minutes to get them hot." The thought of serving eighteen whole crabs was a bit daunting, but that's what we did.

I had asked two young couples, friends of my children, along with my son Craig, who was home from college on vacation, to be the servers. I thought Julia would enjoy young people a lot better than hired caterers. They were absolutely thrilled and did a wonderful job.

So we had crab for the entrée served with a spinach soufflé that didn't fall and some French bread which I made myself. I had never made French bread before, but it turned out to be great.

After that I had to produce finger bowls, because everybody was sticky, fishy from the crab. We had been given a dozen finger bowls as a wedding present, and my neighbor, Ann Powel, who was invited to the party—and being an old Easterner—also had finger bowls and brought over six more.

Then we had a great green salad and a wheel of brie.

At last, it was time for dessert. The dessert had been my biggest problem, my real challenge. Every time I decided what I was going to do, I would be watching Julia Child on her television show and she would have either done that dessert or would be talking about it. Finally, Holt said, "Why don't you just do something you know always turns out well and everybody likes." Excellent advice! So I produced an old family favorite: rum cream pie.

The two white wines we served were a very dry Muscadet and a Pinot Blanc. After the meal we all retired to the living room and had demitasse and liqueurs.

My evening was made when Julia had a second piece of pie.

It was just a wonderful time.

Julia was charming, effusive and very gracious about what everyone had done for her. Her visit was a great highlight in my life—and certainly in my kitchen.

As the years went by, I sometimes visited Smith, being a board member. Julia, who had graduated ten years before I did, often turned up at special occasions for the college as head of culinary and entertainment activities. At these events, Julia and I got to know each other and became friends.

My last remembrance of Julia was in 1998, just before I retired from the board of trustees as chair. Julia was a guest at the president's house, and I was there for some meetings. At breakfast that last morning we finally had a chance to talk. She turned her sparkling eyes on me and said, "Now, Kate, as I remember, you have three children. Tell me about where they are now and what's going on." I could hardly believe it, that after twenty-five years she remembered so much about my family. What you saw is what you got with Julia. It was just so typical of her, one of the most authentic people I've known—charming, unassuming, and so full of life.

A note on the movie, *Julie And Julia*, which came out in 2009: Early on, when I saw the scene where Julia, played by Meryl Streep, walked across the Embassy the first time she was in France, Streep did an amazing job of walking just like Julia—she caught it perfectly! Streep also flawlessly captured Julia's humor, as in the scene where she walked into the cooking class, the only woman in a sea of men. Julia would have loved the movie.

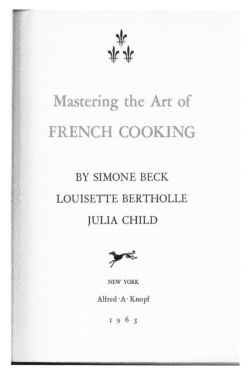

Family Picture Album

Kate, Kelly, Craig, Annie learning to ski at Snoqualmie winter 1959.

February 1972 – Mother and Dad's first party at Kelly and Rob's wedding. Left to right: Dad, me, Mither, and mother.

Ed Platt, Holt, and Jeff Platt, December 1972.

Christmas 1978 – Annie and John's wedding.

Peter and Kelly (top left); Kelly and Nicolas (bottom left); Jenny (top right); Jim, Sarah and Nicolas (bottom right); Jinny and Alex (bottom middle)

Kate's 80th Birthday trip to Rio with Candy Ashmun.

Kelly's And Annie's Weddings

My two daughters each gave me and Holt one month from the time they told us they were engaged to the date they had set for the wedding.

In January of 1972, Kelly called from NYC to say that she and Rob were going to be married in February. I wasn't sure that would be possible, but we pulled it off nonetheless. Kelly was very pleased to wear her great grandmother's wedding dress; it was made for Mrs. John Burns, Holt's grandmother, in Paris around 1888 and already worn by several brides before Kelly. I'm still not quite sure how I inherited this treasure, but my girls had always been enamored by it, hiding in the cedar chest all these years, a two-piece satin dress, adaptable to many sizes. It looked stunning on everybody!

Somehow we managed to get the invitations out to everyone, and had a wonderful wedding in St. Mark's Cathedral, with Annie as the only attendant. The reception was at the Sunset Club.

Kelly horrified the manager of the club by saying she didn't want lots of flowers around but rather wanted balloons. She made this request because she had invited many children for whom she'd baby-sat over the years, and she wanted them to enjoy the party, too! It was a whole new approach at the Sunset Club, but they acquiesced and the reception was a great success.

Annie wore wedding dress from Holt's grandmother, made in Paris in 1888

Several years later Holt and I were in Copenhagen ending up a business trip. It was 5:00 AM on the morning of November 15th, 1978, when the phone rang. Annie announced to us that she and Jon Fox had decided to get married. That in itself was not a great surprise to us. But then she added that they were to be married on the 16th of December. She reassured us that she had arranged everything. "I have the church," she told us—St. Barnabas, Bainbridge Island. "I have the minister. We would like the reception to be at Sunnybranch. And I have made up the guest list. Also," she continued, "I'm not going to wear great grandmother's wedding dress. And Kelly is going to be my only attendant."

I took a deep breath and said, "Annie, I don't have my address book with me, or my rolodex or anything else. But if I make a list of people which I hope you included on your list, would you be willing to look at that and discuss it with me in case you forgot somebody?"

"Yes, certainly," she said.

When we got home I made up my guest list. As it happened, when Annie and I compared lists, there were only three people on mine that weren't on hers—and they were all older generation people whom she was very pleased to include.

Again, we pulled off a wonderful wedding. A great success. In getting ready for the wedding, we tried to find a tent, it being winter and we felt we couldn't host 150 comfortably in the house. But we couldn't find an adequate tent that could be attached as an extension of the house. So Holt, Johnny Powel, Don King and Vern Williams—plus help from the younger generation, Carl Williams, Craig, Jeff Powel, etc.—covered our swimming pool! It took three days to pull off, and was a tremendous amount of work. In the end, we had a wonderful temporary floor over the pool. A small band was set up there, and Junkoh Harui from Bainbridge Gardens loaned us all kinds of plants, so it looked like a real wedding bower, adding greatly to the festivities!

It turns out a wedding can be done in a month. I don't recommend it to anyone. But it's possible. A footnote: In the end, Annie did plan to wear her great grandmother's dress. It was a lovely addition to the ceremony, and Holt and I were very pleased that she had made that decision.

Annie's Graduation. Left to right: Annie, mother, dad, me, and Holt.

Craig's Graduation. Left to right: me, Craig, Dad, mother.

Tlingit Totem Pole Preserved At Sunnybranch

We purchased this Tlingit totem pole from Joe James, owner of "The Old Curiosity Shop" in Seattle – he inherited the shop from his grandfather.

In 1978, Joe called us about a totem pole sale, knowing we were interested. It was in-between Kelly's and Annie's wedding that this opportunity presented itself to us. There was to be an auction of old, genuine poles. There was one in particular Joe believed we would like.

So Holt and I attended the auction. In typical Holt fashion, my husband said, "I've never been to an auction where I was actually going to buy something. I should practice first." So he bought a canoe. Then an old rail road bell. The bell hangs in the patio and the children still love to ring it.

Finally the Tlingit totem pole came up, and before too long we had purchased it. The beautiful artwork stands at the back door of our Sunnybranch home.

Part III

The Professional Volunteer

In the early 1950s, I learned of a new development in the commercial world that I felt could affect me in many positive ways. My news came from *Frederick & Nelson*, the department store which at that time had decided that married women could get credit cards in their own names. Up until that point we'd all been "Mrs. Somebody—" I'd been Mrs. Holt W. Webster.

So one day I mentioned this development to Holt, and he, in his characteristic way said, "Do you think that's necessary?"

I answered, "Yes."

And he said, "Okay."

Thus, I applied for and received my first, very own credit card.

In those early Newton Street years, I was learning how to keep house, how to be a mother—I'm still learning that one!—and how to be a supportive and loving wife to Holt as he started his new business.

One day, my neighbor Edith Williams, came to visit. She was ten years older than I, and had moved to Seattle from New York with her lawyer husband. Edith was also a dedicated volunteer. Her grandfather being Theodore Roosevelt, it was quite natural for her to became involved in Republican politics. Edith said that it was time for me to get involved in community affairs and as she needed help with precinct work that would be a good place for me to start. As I cast my first presidential vote for Eisenhower, precinct work seemed to be a way to learn—and so I did.

After almost two years of being involved in very basic jobs, it was clear that politics was not my cup of tea. There seemed to be no room for disagreement or pro-and-con discussions, and the concept of "expediency" dominated decision-making. There are many ways to describe expediency, but the shortest is Webster's: "A temporary means to an end." The concept was not one I could accept and so ended my political involvement. Edith and I remained friends, however, and years later we served together as Regents at Washington State University.

As life became routine and as our children began school, I grew more and more aware of all that was going on in our community and in the greater Seattle area. Friends who had the time were volunteers in many different areas. They seemed to be welcomed by a growing number of agencies and institutions.

Philanthropy was never a word that came trippingly off my tongue, but the words "giving" and "time, talent and treasure" were an integral part of our childhood. Mother and Dad, starting as young physicians in New York City during the Depression, gave freely of their time to indigent patients and continued this practice throughout their careers.

My Grandmother Kate Fuller Belcher volunteered in Newark, New Jersey Public Schools in the 1920s and continued her volunteering as the first president of Planned Parenthood in New Jersey in 1927, also serving on the first national board.

Mrs. MacIntosh, head of Brearley School, was way ahead of her time. In the late 1930s, as junior high students, we were required to spend one afternoon weekly caring for and working with children in a nearby neighborhood center whom we called "latch-key kids." In college, I continued some volunteering, but it was sporadic.

Given that background, when friends asked me to join the Junior League Of Seattle, it seemed to be the ideal way to learn about the region and explore the many areas open to volunteers. So, six years and three children after my arrival in Seattle, I began my first intensive volunteer commitment.

The Junior League Of Seattle (founded in 1923) required a six week training course, four long days a week. Thanks to my friends who often filled in as sitters, we all survived this volunteer "boot camp."

The Junior League also gave me, a newcomer to the Northwest, a unique introduction to the city and an unrivaled opportunity to become part of an exciting, growing community. The combined experience of League administration and volunteer activity established a base which has enabled me to participate in a wide range of civic, health, welfare, and education organizations.

In those days we had lots of placement choices (some menial scutwork, some creative, and some challenging). We had to work three or four hours every week. It was a great exposure to such agencies as the Seattle Art Museum, Harborview Medical Center, the Council On Aging, the Gilbert & Sullivan Society, Seattle Day Nursery (now Childhaven), Seattle Children's Home, and the Junior League's Children's Theatre, which "toured" to Seattle Public Schools.

This decade of hands-on volunteering taught us a lot about Seattle, about people, and about what a difference volunteers can make. We also had fund raising events, such as the Follies and the Thrift Shop (started on my Board watch). The shop was a "group" philanthropy, but we all learned how to give. Personal donations were small, but the total gave us a huge boost.

There followed, through the Junior League, a series of short, one-to-three year board memberships (see list in Addendum 5). Each was a valuable learning experience and an exposure to different parts of the Seattle community as well as a great way to meet people, make friends, and begin to understand all the institutions, agencies and civic groups that make up our fair city. Coming from New York City, I was struck early on by the encouragement and acceptance of Seattleites to try something new. People fifty years ago and still today have been willing to look at fresh ideas or new approaches to situations that are outdated or no longer of value. In that sense, the Puget Sound area was and still is an exciting place to live.

We have all heard friends discuss their long range plans. I've never been good at that—possibly because something always happened to change my ideas. So I would just wait to see what developed, and other areas opened up. Quite honestly I believed most opportunities occurred because of the people I met while volunteering at Children's, WSU Board Of Regents, Lakeside School Board, Seafirst Bank, and the Seattle Foundation Board, all of which became part of my volunteer life. I've also been fortunate to have had a whole host of wonderful, rewarding, learning, and challenging experiences. And through it all, I have made so many good and lasting friendships along with a broad exposure to the world of philanthropy.

One extraordinary and unique experience of my volunteer career was the founding of City Club in 1980—extraordinary, because of eight former Junior League volunteers who met at a lunch one day and decided we should keep in touch.

The History Of CITYCLUB
[source: http://www.seattlecityclub.org/history]

In 1980, eight women seeking to contribute to the community's civic dialogue got together to form the nucleus of CityClub in Seattle. At the time, many civic organizations, such as Rotary International, were open to men only. The founders of CityClub determined that the new organization would be open to all and would provide a nonpartisan forum for ideas and debate. Since its first presentation in 1981, the organization has sponsored hundreds of dialogues, discussions, and debates from local, regional, and national experts and leaders. A co-sponsor of the annual Jefferson Awards, CityClub is recognized as one of the region's foremost civic and public affairs organizations.

After 26 years of programming, CityClub remains committed to its founding vision – providing a welcoming forum for civic discourse on the most critical issues of the moment. CityClub programs are non-partisan, pluralistic, and accessible to all.

CityClub Founders: Anne V. Farrell, Barbara M. Hodgson, Suzanne F. Lile (now Hunter), Nancy S. Nordhoff, Jean B. Rolfe, Marilyn B. Ward, Kate B. Webster, Colleen S. Willoughby

We had all been Junior League volunteers, but our paths had split. We met for a 7:30 breakfast every month for two years, and then decided that our networking had meant so much to us that there were probably others who could benefit from the same experience. So we founded City Club, a place for young professionals to meet and become informed and involved in our city.

Many of our friends thought we were crazy, but Seattle was and is still a city receptive to new ideas. I've learned never be afraid or hesitant to "go for it." And the big plus is that the eight of us (now called "OGs" for "Old Girls") are still best buddies and have breakfast as often as we can get together.

Besides the three main arenas of volunteer opportunity I enjoyed—Children's Hospital, WSU, and Smith College—I also spent time working on a number of other non-profit boards.

To mention a few, The Council On Aging was my first board experience. At the time I missed my grandmother and her contemporaries, many of whom had been role models as I was growing up. The Council On Aging was new. The whole subject of geriatrics was evolving in the early 1950s, and I was pleased to be "the youngster" on that board. The leadership was aggressive and set out to educate Seattle on the needs of older people. For me, my ability to keep up with the learning curve developed rapidly as did the friendships.

Jean B. Rolfe, Suzanne F. Lile (now Hunter), Barbara M Hodgson, Marilyn B. Ward, Nancy S. Nordhoff, Anne V. Farrell, Colleen S. Willoughby, Kate B. Webster

The Seattle Day Nursery, which has evolved into "Childhaven," exposed me to the other end of the spectrum of needs. It was on that Board that I began to understand the plight of neglected, abused children as well as those with physical and emotional needs who had little or no hope of assistance. One other lesson from my time serving Seattle Day Nursery turned out to be an extremely valuable addition to my growing list of Board experiences. Some months after we had hired a new executive director, the Board found itself split on a crucial issue. The director had fired a staff member. Almost all the male trustees felt this was not an authorized action, and they wanted to dismiss the director. The women trustees unanimously disagreed, believing that hiring and firing staff was the director's responsibility, not that of the Board. After a long and heated discussion all the men except one walked out, never to be seen again. The lone male, Paul Langpaap, respected Rector of Trinity Episcopal Parish at the time, clapped his hands and said, "It's OK. Now, let's get back to work."

The post-war period was a time of much change in the operation of non-profits. Boards had traditionally been "where the buck stopped," but as more and more trained professionals came on the scene it became apparent that the operational "chief" should be in charge of all paid staff. Today everyone accepts this as gospel. But the process did take a while to evolve.

Some years later, in the mid-1970s, I was invited to join the Board of the Bloedel Reserve. The Bloedels had decided to open their beautiful Bainbridge property to the public, and I represented the "locals." It was a privilege to watch Mr. Bloedel guide us through all the steps of his plan and a treat to get to know him as a friend. He was a thoughtful, brilliant organizer with a gentle but determined approach to his strategy for the reserve. Early on he decided to deed the property to the University of Washington, with stipulations that it be available for public enjoyment. When the university failed to fulfill his requirements, Mr. Bloedel bought it back, an amazing feat! He was a diplomat as well as an astute businessman, and everything worked out just as he had planned. The Bloedel Reserve continues to be a popular destination stop on Bainbridge Island.

The Maytime Ball

In early 1957 I was invited to lunch with Ann Bucknall and fifteen friends. Her phone message ended with, "You'll be sorry if you don't show up."

Of course I went. And I joined the others there to discuss the possibilities of producing a springtime ball for our generation. The Four original planners had decided that since we were at that age—too old to be invited to a Christmas Ball, and too young to afford individual dance parties—we decided to put on a springtime celebration. We called it the "Maytime Ball."

The party was always held at the elegant Fairmont Olympic Hotel on University Street in Seattle. (Interestingly, the Olympic first opened its doors in 1924, the year I was born.)

Jim and Aimee Sten Crissey, who owned their own flower shop on Market Street, provided the decorations from start to finish. Many friendships were made and kept, as we organized each event.

After our first ball, some of the committee stayed and helped Jim Crissey clean up. There were always pink hydrangeas, which were the major decoration. Jim suggested we might take them home. Today I still have several hydrangea bushes—though they've now turned blue.

We continued the celebration for many years, well into the 1990s. We held the last one, in the

The Committee of

The Maytime Ball

requests the pleasure of

Mr. and Mrs. Webster's

company at

The Olympic Hotel

on Friday evening, the 13th of May

at ten o'clock

R.s.v.p. by May 9th
The Maytime Ball
407 94th S.E.   Formal
Bellevue, Washington 98004   Subscription $20 per person

You are invited to join us for a no-host dinner
at the Olympic Hotel before The Ball

Mr. and Mrs. William D. Bowden
Mr. and Mrs. Minor C. Lile, Jr.
Mr. and Mrs. G. Anton Mueller

If interested, R.s.v.p. by May 9th
to Mrs. J. Fergus McRee - 322-2991

late 90s, reluctantly deciding that there were so few limber men to whirl us around that it was time to move on to quieter activities.

Betty Bottler continued as our ongoing president, and those members who are still around have tried to meet for an annual lunch.

Committee

Mr. and Mrs. Gilbert W. Anderson
Mr. and Mrs. Robert J. Behnke
Mr. and Mrs. William Darsie Bowden
Mr. and Mrs. Irving M. Clark, Jr.
Mrs. Taber Jenkins
Doctor and Mrs. Donald Lewis
Mr. and Mrs. Minor C. Lile, Jr.
Mr. and Mrs. G. Anton Mueller
Mr. and Mrs. Carl Henry Neu
Mrs. Purcell Park
Mr. and Mrs. John Hare Powel
Mr. and Mrs. Andrew Price, Jr.
Mr. and Mrs. John Rolfe
Mr. and Mrs. Roe Duke Watson
Mr. and Mrs. Holt Wilson Webster
Mr. and Mrs. Bagley Wright

My Years At Children's Hospital

After years of writing "housewife" as my occupation on various forms, I decided that "professional volunteer" was really my job.

After eleven years of volunteering, under the auspices of the Junior League Of Seattle, a whole new world of opportunities opened up. It didn't take long to learn the obvious: there was a limit to the number of community responsibilities one could handle. A few challenging spot jobs were always possible, as they had a beginning and an end—search committees, fundraising affairs, a panel discussion or a specific church fundraiser. These all came my way and could somehow be scheduled. But the majority of my volunteer activities for the next thirty-four years centered around three institutions, Children's Hospital, Washington State University, and Smith College.

Retired from the Junior League at forty, as was required in my day, I had no clue as to what my next volunteer job would be. To my great surprise and delight, I was asked to be on the Children's Orthopedic Hospital Board. For twelve years, that's all I did. It was a full time commitment which I loved and felt very lucky to have. In those days the Board really was in charge—i.e., the buck stopped there!

The depth of experience as a Board member of "Children's"—as it is called today—was fulfilling and rewarding. (My 31 years, which would be an unheard of tenure in today's world, has provided me with a vivid picture of the rapidly changing world of medicine along with the growth of amazing technology and its effects on healthcare.)

My first seven years at Children's Orthopedic Hospital (its original name), was a huge learning curve. My initial job was oversight of "membership." There were 500 plus guilds in the state, mostly in King County, but there was a scattering of them in almost every county. Each spring and fall, the more remote guilds expected a visit from "The Board"—a formidable task.

Thanks to Ruth Wakefeld, then president of the board, I survived. Ruth and I traveled over every mountain pass and to all corners of the state. As a newcomer to the Northwest, I had never been east of the mountains, every trip was an escapade. Ruth had a delightful sense of humor and a "lead foot" on the gas pedal; luckily in all our years of driving she only got one speeding ticket.

The guilds we met were of varying sizes—some almost one hundred members and occasionally a few very small groups. I wondered about the importance of traveling, for example, to a small town in the Okanagan Valley to find only six ladies waiting there for us. It was, however, one of our most memorable visits. Three of them had had children in the hospital, and all were grateful for the care they received, generous in their support, and eager to hear all the latest news. The Seattle area guilds kept me busy at home, while committee work in Seattle opened up new vistas of the challenges and complexities of running a hospital.

In 1970 I was elected chair of the Board of Trustees, and I began one of the most memorable experiences of my life. As we learned about Children's Hospitals throughout the country, it became clear that those of us who were "free-standing"—that is, who had no formal relationship with a teaching hospital—would neither survive financially nor be able to keep up nearly as well with the new technical developments in the medical world.

Therefore, we began to discuss the possibilities of affiliation with the leaders of the University of Washington and their medical school. After four years of ongoing discussions on many levels of both hospital and university leadership, we finalized an affiliation agreement. Governing boards of both institutions signed the document in December of 1974. It took at least another decade to resolve the many thorny issues; territories, personalities, and finances—all had to be worked out. As in so many similar relationships, almost a total replacement of personnel took place before the process was completed.

Dr. Jack Docter, medical director of Children's, and Dr. Robert van Citters, Dean of the U.W. Medical School, both provided superb leadership and held fast to our goal until the process was completed.

In 1979 the board hired its first CEO, Treuman Katz.[1] Gradually we began to see a more smoothly operating, professionally trained staff. All were coping with chronic and acute illnesses, new technology, and the ever rising costs of medical care.

Board tenure at Children's was always interesting, challenging, and rewarding. Everyone, professional and lay staff, volunteers, parents and patients, all believed that miracles could be accomplished. And, indeed, they continue to happen. The miracle for me is to have been part of Children's during some of its most exciting years!

Entrance to Hospital Complex

1   https://www.seattlechildrens.org/research/centers-programs/bioethics/about/

CHILDREN'S ORTHOPEDIC HOSPITAL AND
MEDICAL CENTER/UNIVERSITY OF WASHINGTON

Agreement of Financial Arrangements

The Children's Orthopedic Hospital and Medical Center and the University
of Washington have entered into an Affiliation Agreement, dated
October 1, 1974, to develop and provide joint health sciences education,
research and patient care programs. This Affiliation Agreement
acknowledges that the differentiated financial obligations for these
joint health sciences programs would be covered by a separate financial
agreement. Pursuant to the terms of the Affiliation Agreement, each
institution intends to provide financial support to each joint health
science program in proportion to the contribution of the program to
the respective institution's stated goals. It is the intent of the
institutions that the cost-finding and cost-apportionment scheme
should 1) be inclusive of all health sciences related joint costs,
2) provide incentives for the development and operation of high
quality, minimum cost joint health science programs, and 3) provide
an uncomplicated and administratively inexpensive routine cost-finding
and cost apportionment process.

APPROVED:

THE CHILDREN'S ORTHOPEDIC
HOSPITAL AND MEDICAL CENTER

BY: *Kate B. Webster*

TITLE: *Chairman Board of Trustees*

DATE: *January 8 1975*

THE UNIVERSITY
OF WASHINGTON

BY: _____
JACK G. NEUPERT

TITLE: PRESIDENT, BOARD OF REGENTS

DATE: *Dec. 16, 1974*

Approved as to form;

Gerald L. Coe
Assistant Attorney General
State of Washington

102

Kate and Dr. Jack Docter

Mom, Emilie Schrabacher, Francis Owen, Treuman Katz

Washington State University

In early 1975, Frances Owen, whom I still called Mrs. Owen at that point, asked me over for tea. It was nearing the end of my tenure as chair of the board of Children's Hospital, and as Mrs. Owen had been my teacher, mentor and friend for the past decade, I of course accepted, with only a slight concern about what had gone wrong. Francis was fourteen years older than I and had been a leader in many civic organizations for years. She was just retiring as a Regent at WSU (Washington State University), and reported to me that she had suggested to Governor Dan Evans that I be appointed to replace her. I was astounded!

Never having been to Pullman, knowing much more about the University of Washington in Seattle than about the WSU, and having been indoctrinated by all my Husky friends to the greater importance of the UW, the question that came to mind was: *Why would I want to do that?* Frances smiled, more graciously than I deserved, and explained that her years at WSU were both challenging and fascinating, and that WSU was a far better school than "Westsiders" knew. Finally, she told me that I would not only learn a lot but could draw on my different education, namely private, all-girls schools, and thus bring a different perspective to the university.

So, that July, Pullman became my second home—nine years serving with Glenn Terrell and nine years with Sam Smith, the two WSU presidents while I was on the board.

The first few years, my learning curve was steep and unpredictable. We met for two days, ten months of every year, mostly in Pullman but occasionally in summer at a farm, vineyard, or city somewhere in Eastern Washington. In the fall, we also always met with the UW Regents during the annual Apple Cup football game between the WSU and the UW.

In the late 70s and 80s, students became vocal and tested the administration to see how many changes they could effect. Glenn Terrell, known as "the student's president," was very patient. His psychology background and wry sense of humor succeed, almost always, in keeping the campus reasonably calm. The eruption of Mount St. Helens in May 1980 was a case in point. The campus was covered in ash, classes were canceled, and students advised to stay in their dorms. Glenn handled the situation in a masterful fashion, even coping with frantic parents and groping and grasping media.

Sam Smith took over as president in 1985. The importance of a higher education was being recognized in a public fashion more than ever before in the State of Washington. Sam was instrumental in developing a closer relationship with the UW. One of the accomplishments of which he was most proud was that, during his tenure, the WSU grew tremendously in size, and as a result more than a third of the total number of graduates were matriculated and became part of the Alumni Association.

Both Presidents Terrell and Smith communicated easily and often with all the regents. Board meetings were attended by students and faculty as well as the administrative staff. Everyone felt empowered to ask questions and, from time to time, to disagree. The sessions were lively, and reaching a consensus was always the goal.

I grew to love "the Palouse" (a geographic area covering some 10,000 square miles of northwestern Idaho and southeastern Washington). Each season brought a new view of the fields and mountains, and over the years, as a WSU Regent, our meetings took us all over the state.

I'm proud to be an adopted Cougar and am so fortunate to have made many good friends throughout the Northwest.

Kate Webster and her mother Dr. Anne Belcher Note: The citation on the Physical Sciences Building reads "18 Years" of service. Actually, Kate served for 19 years, because Governor Booth Gardner forgot to replace her!

Smith College Board

In 1985, when I was still a Regent at WSU, Smith College elected me to a five year term as "Alumna Trustee." Holt had just retired, and I thought there was enough on my plate, but he encouraged me to accept. Mom and Dad were still living in New York City, and the trips east would provide opportunities to visit them. So I started traveling once again to Northampton, Massachusetts.

My first meeting was also the beginning of Mary Dunn's tenure as the new college president. At Mary's inauguration, Smith alumna, Julia Child, had been asked to oversee the party held in the Quadrangle's open courtyard. The food was fabulous and Julia was charming.

Those five years passed quickly, and it was interesting to contrast the differences between the Smith campus and that of WSU. I discovered that there were more similarities than I had at first envisioned. Faculty, students, administration, and alumni are essentially the same everywhere. The big difference was where the financing came from and how it was handled. The lack of "political red tape" at Smith was refreshing.

At the end of my five years at Smith, I came home and found the next two years to be more relaxing. Children's and WSU were still in my life, but I had no major responsibilities and much more time to enjoy "retirement" with Holt. He even talked me into playing a little "beginner's golf."

Holt's sudden illness and unexpected death in April 1992 was devastating. Children, grand-children, extended family and friends kept me going—but the question of what would I do and how would I rebuild my life was ever-present. I knew that I was not unique, but those first months alone are always tough.

A phone call in October of '92 astounded me and made a huge difference in my life in so many ways. It was from one of my Smith trustee friends, Don Hood, chair of the Board nominating committee. He informed me the Board had nominated me as Chair elect—this would mean another five year term. The timing was wonderful, and the thought of returning to an institution where I knew so many people, and with whom I had a long-standing relationship was heartwarming.

The following five years were extremely difficult in some ways but were among the most fulfilling in others. My Board tenure at both Children's and WSU came to a close—and it was time. But it's never easy to say "goodbye" after so many great years.

At Smith, the Board of Trustees was charged with searching for and hiring a new president for the college. We appointed a great committee made up of eight trustees, four faculty members and two students who were juniors. Working hard for nine months, we were thrilled to hire Ruth Simmons, at that time acting provost at Princeton. Ruth was the first African-American woman to head a major university, let alone an Ivy League college, in the USA—and she was superb. Working with her for the next three years was a treat and a great educational experience.

My retirement the spring of 1998 marked the end of my "full time" Board commitments. I was very fortunate, learned an enormous amount, and formed so many wonderful friendships over the years. No one could ask for more.

That fall, I was appointed Chair of the Smith College medal committee—a five year job that led to meeting many incredibly talented and successful Smith alumnae from all over the country. They represented a vast spectrum of professions, volunteer activities, and cultural traditions. We awarded four or five medals a year, which were recognized at our annual "Rally Day" celebra-

Kate and Ruth Simmons at 50th Class Reunion

Kate and Ruth Simmons at 50th Class Reunion

Kate receiving John M. Green Award at Smith College, 1999

tions in February. These Smithies ranged in age from recent grads to several who had already enjoyed their 50th reunions. Meeting them, listening to their stories, and having a chance to visit one-on-one afforded me many unforgettable experiences with these extraordinary women.

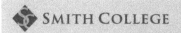

The John M. Greene Award

Kate Belcher Webster '46: For more than 55 years, you have responded enthusiastically and unhesitatingly to every need of Smith College. You served as Chair of the Board of Trustees, Alumnae Trustee, President of the Smith College Club of Seattle and, at present, Chair of the Medal Committee. You are an unparalleled example of dedicated service to Smith College.

Your career as a volunteer began upon graduation from Smith, when the Class of 1946 needed a fund agent. You took the job simply because you were asked to do it. Thus began a personal tradition of keeping in touch with Smith graduates throughout their lives and throughout the world.

Moving to Seattle in 1947 with your husband, Holt, you quickly became involved with the Smith College Club of Seattle. Over the years—while you skied and sailed, cooked creative casseroles and drove countless carpools for your three children—you also served as the elected president of this active Seattle Smith Club. Deeply involved in your community in many capacities, you were regarded as a dependable and decisive leader of the local Smith alumnae.

In 1985, while serving as chair of the Board of Regents of Washington State University, you were elected as an Alumnae Trustee at Smith. Your first Board meeting was also the first for the newly appointed president, Mary Maples Dunn. Your judgment and experience were invaluable as the College plotted its course for the future. Having your granddaughter, Sarah, at Smith while you were serving on the Board was fun for both of you and provided lively insights into what was really happening on campus, as well as another link to the college that both your sister, Suzanne, and your daughter, Anne, attended.

Although your five-year term as Alumnae Trustee ended, your work on the Board was so outstanding that you were called back three years later as Chair-Elect. Once again, you embarked on those pre-dawn flights from the West Coast to the East for the myriad meetings and strategy sessions. Your hearty laugh and the twinkle in your dark eyes enhanced your leadership skills as listener, evaluator and humanist concerned about all members of the college community.

As Chair of the Board, you exemplified skilled leadership while regularly facing challenging issues, all the time keeping a sharp eye on costs. You helped Smith find Ruth Simmons, its ninth president. You became her partner and launched Smith into its next brilliant chapter. With Ruth as president and you as Chair, Smith embarked on a major institutional self-study that culminated in ambitious objectives, including the engineering program, the Praxis program and the Kahn Liberal Arts Institute. You oversaw the Campus Center feasibility study and the decision to renovate and expand the Fine Arts Center, building projects that are now coming to fruition. You planted and nurtured so many seeds from which the institution now reaps benefits.

Kate, the breadth and depth of your commitment to Smith College are remarkable. It is with deep gratitude that the Board of Trustees presents to you the John M. Greene Award for distinguished service to Smith College.

Rochelle B. Lazarus

Rochelle Braff Lazarus '68, *Chair, Board of Trustees*
February 20, 2003

The Bishop Foundation

In 2000, my close friend Janet Skadan called and said she had a job for me. She had been a valued trustee of the "Bishop Foundation" since the beginning in 1972; but Parkinson's' Disease had taken its toll, and she felt she could no longer serve. She recommended me to the board, of only two others, and they asked me to join.

Jim Newton's Helicopter, 2006 Bishop Foundation Committee Hood Canal Trip

Three trustees and a wonderful lawyer, who served as staff, were charged with managing and fulfilling the rules laid down by Mr. Bishop. He had decreed that the foundation should be "sunsetted" after twenty-five years, so I had one year of normal operation and then five years to dispose of all the assets.

Isabelle Lamb and Jim Mason, both from the Aberdeen-Grays Harbor area, were the other two trustees, and Tom Nevers provided all the necessary information. The funds were all dedicated to public service, and most of the awards went to the Grays Harbor area, but other institutions also benefited, especially in the Seattle area.

The Island School

The Island School, known to many as Kelly's School, was a vital part of our history. In 2008, Island School's Webster Hall was dedicated, and I was asked to speak.

"What a wonderful day, one that we have all been anticipating for a long time. My only regret is that Holt is not here to share it with us. The story of the Island School from our point of view starts this way: On a quiet winter weekend, nearly 32 years ago, Kelly dropped by and announced she had some exciting news—'Nancy and David Leedy and I want to start an elementary school on Bainbridge Island', she said, 'and we need your help and advice'."

This was how it all began. Holt and I looked at one another, took a deep breath and asked for further details. We obviously had no idea what we'd be getting into! But we were impressed with their thoughtful planning, their passion and their vision. And, as a streak of entrepreneurship seems to run in the Webster family, along with a strong belief in the importance of a challenging, comprehensive *and* individually supportive education, we agreed to share with Kelly our experiences in the non-profit world.

We never dreamed, of course, that this would be a life-long relationship. But here we are. Our family is very proud of Kelly's and her colleagues' dedication through the years, as they built a solid foundation which would transform students' potential from dreams into realities, offering them a living, exciting place to grow and to thrive. Without their steady, visionary work through those thirty-one years, we wouldn't be here, celebrating the School's past success and planning for its future.

David Leedy, Kelly Webster, Nancy Leedy

This building, Webster Hall, was part of Kelly's dream from the beginning, and my family and I welcome this opportunity to share with her in our community's future. All the basics had to come first, and now its completion opens opportunities for new generations of Island School students and their creative faculty and staff.

To Trish and her team, our hearty congratulations. We foresee the Hall as a creative source, a home, for both the school and the community, and as the birthplace of new ideas and cooperative ventures for years to come.

Grace Church

GRACE CHURCH   WEBSTER CHAPEL

Grace Church has been a part of my life forever—not this Grace Church, Bainbridge Island, to be sure—but my mother and father were married in Grace Episcopal Church in New Jersey.

So, decades later as a group of us gathered on Bainbridge Island to establish a new Episcopal Church, the proposed name "Grace" really resonated for me. It immediately meant fellowship and community, a place to refresh my soul and to retain and further develop my belief in and connection with God. A place that felt like home.[1]

In our early days, as we adopted our four major tenets of "inclusion, service, discovery, and gratitude"—this in itself was a long and somewhat noisy process—but as we reached consensus, I think we all felt a growing sense of belonging to a church community we could believe in, be a part of, and support as it grew.

Now, after 22 years in our building, we are a parish and Grace continues to sustain us all. From our baptismal font to our memorial garden we continue to learn and understand that each stage of life is an integral part of our community.

1   Architectural photo courtesy of James Cutler, Cutler Anderson Architects.

But even as I stand here feeling blessed and cared for and more than a little humble, I realized that Grace is also a business. Our beautiful building needs to be maintained, our staff—both clerical and lay—deserves to be well cared for. And our countless expectations, such as light, heat, grounds-keeping, outstanding programs, and of course coffee service and treats (to name just a few) require constant attention.

Our first priest, Reverend Bill Harper, has just taken early retirement. His 20-plus years of service to the Grace community has been unique and exciting, with changes to liturgy and programs. Bill's strengths, and his greatest gift to Grace, were the development of programs which formed a strong relationship with parish youth. And also Bill's sermons shined! Somehow he always made his homilies relevant to today's world and managed to inject just the right amount of humor.

Grace's 10 acres of land, which had been originally clear-cut, was a challenge to develop. But the property has become a wonderful spot for both church and community activities.

2015, we have just hired our new priest, Tommy J. Dillon II, and look forward to another "Grace" adventure. Originally from Louisiana, Tommy also served eight years in San Francisco. He is a people-person and interested in the whole Island community. Tommy is eager to learn about and connect with Island life, and he is looking forward to becoming an important part of Grace Church.

Kate B. Webster Medical Pavilion Children's Hospital

In early June 2016 I received a call from Doug Picha at Children's Hospital. He asked me if he and Dr. Jeff Sperring, our new hospital CEO, could come to visit because he had a question for me. To my astonishment he announced that they wanted to name the new section of the hospital the "Kate B. Webster Medical Pavilion."

The dedication was held on June 22nd, celebrating this new place where Children's Hospital staff and University Of Washington physicians could meet and plan together. This honor was a huge surprise for me, wrapped up as it was with memories of 31 years as a hospital trustee!

Kate with great grandchildren, Nicolas, MaryKate, and Chase

Lessons Of Being A Professional Volunteer

I have learned—as you all will—that volunteer experience builds self-confidence. You learn to trust your instincts. And if you have a "nag" don't write it off. Check the pros and cons, ask as many questions as you need to before making decisions, and—above all as a leader—keep your board informed.

The most successful board experience comes when there is a strong positive relationship between the Board and the CEO or Head or President, based on a shared vision, open communication, trust and common goals. None of us is born with these skills, but when an Administrator and Board can work together as a team, it all begins to fall into place.

Volunteering has truly been my profession. The experience has always been quite wonderful, and actually still is. Volunteering and taking risks when everything points to the need is challenging, fulfilling, and rewarding.

Philanthropy, donating our assets as well as we can, is an important part of a volunteer life. It's personal and certainly varies as life changes. But both volunteerism and philanthropy are part—or should be—of everyone's contributions in life. The amounts of time, talent and treasure to give will vary, but, often, even a smile or a helping hand can make a big difference in other's lives.

Finally, don't spend time anticipating all the problems and headaches and occasional heartaches. They will come and you will cope. The joy and satisfaction is in the doing and in knowing that you can and do make a difference.

A life of
volunteer
work/C1

Section C

Monday
September 23, 1985
Seattle Post-Intelligencer

To define 'volunteers,' just look up the Websters

By Don Carter
P-I Reporter

"We were going to travel," says Holt Webster, "but somehow that hasn't happened yet."

Webster retired 17 months ago as chairman and chief executive officer of Airborne Freight Corp., but it will be another couple of months before he and his wife, Kate, can fit travel into their plans.

Their combined schedule, which is packed with commitments to civic, educational and other organizations, is why the Bainbridge Island couple have been named recipients of the YMCA's A.K. Guy Award for community service. The award, named for the late president of G.O. Guy drugstores, will be presented at a YMCA luncheon at the Westin Hotel tomorrow.

The Websters' community service began as a way of getting acquainted in a new community shortly after they were married in 1947. Kate is a native of New York, and Holt is a Portland, Ore., native. They met in Portland at the wedding of Kate's Smith College roommate, and "after six dates over six months decided to get married," Holt says.

Holt and Kate Webster

Kate was the first to become involved in volunteer work, "because we really knew no one in Seattle," she says. During the couple's early years in Seattle, Holt had no time for anything but his fledgling business, Pacific Air Freight, which later merged with Airborne Freight. He recalls that during

those early years, he routinely rounded up business all day and then spent his evenings delivering the freight to the airport.

Kate describes her volunteer activities as "an evolutionary thing. One thing led to another. In the early days, I tried a number of different volunteer experiences, and although I found them all challenging, I got to the point where I had to limit myself. You can't do it all." So today she pretty much specializes in health and educational causes.

Her early service began with the Junior League, an organization devoted to volunteer work, and in 1963 she was invited to join the board of directors of Children's Orthopedic Hospital. She later became president of the board. "Both of my parents are doctors, so I've always had an interest in health," she says.

It was Frances Owen, a colleague on the hospital board, who persuaded Kate to join the Washington State University Board of Regents in 1976. "I'd never even been to Pullman," Kate says. "But Frances thought it was wonderful, and I thought that if she

See COUPLE, Page C-2

From Page C-1

felt that way it would certainly be fascinating for me."

Along the way, she served on the boards of the Council on Aging, Seattle Day Nursery, United Way of King County, Bloedel Foundation, Seattle Foundation, YMCA of Greater Seattle, CityClub, St. Nicholas and Lakeside schools, Northwest Kidney Foundation, and the National Association of Children's Hospitals. She also has been active in a number of Episcopal Church organizations on both the parish and diocesan levels.

And her volunteer experience led to an invitation in 1975 to become the first woman on the Seafirst Bank board of directors.

Holt joined his wife on the volunteer circuit in 1970, when arts activist Ned Skinner made him the head of fund-raising for the United Arts Fund. Holt is proud of Airborne Freight's track record of financial support for arts and civic causes. "When you grow to a certain size, you get to the point where you should give something back to the community." His zeal for community service led to board and fund-raising work for Children's Orthopedic Hospital, the Citizens Council Against Crime, the YMCA Capital Campaign, Independent Colleges of Washington, and United Way of King County. Holt also has served as president of the Seattle Chamber of Commerce and on the vestry of St. Mark's Cathedral.

Both Websters are pleased by what they perceive as a "turning around" in the drop-off of volunteer activity which followed the trend toward two-career couples. Women, who traditionally have borne the larger share of volunteer work, have had to devote more time and energy to jobs.

But Holt believes that as soon as couples get settled in their two-job lifestyles, they will return to volunteer activity. "There's a point where they start to realize there's more to life than just going to the

office every day," he says. "I think they need other outlets for their energy."

Kate, who was one of founders of CityClub, says that the organization's purpose has been to introduce downtown professionals to volunteer needs of the community through regular lunch-hour programs on health, educational and arts issues, and other activities.

Although Holt "resigned from two or three volunteer activities, and then took on another one" (presidency of the Seattle Central Community College Foundation) when he retired, he has no plans to change his lifestyle. He remains a director of Airborne Freight, Puget Sound Power and Light and Washington Mutual Savings Bank.

"I'm busy, but I'm also finding time for some retirement," he says. "I'm learning to build a barn, learning to garden, learning to do things around the house, and taking up golf again after 40 years.

"We're also doing a lot of baby-sitting," he adds. The couple now has five grandchildren. And they have finally scheduled some travel, a trip to Strasbourg, France, later this fall to visit the oldest of their three children and her family.

Although Kate has tried to limit her activities, she recently accepted a position on the board of trustees of her alma mater. The job will require four trips a year to Smith College in Northampton, Mass.

But, she notes, it also will let her visit her parents in New York more frequently. Her father, now 92, has retired, but her mother, 89, still works 5½ days a week at her ear, nose and throat practice.

Kate laughs and shakes her head when asked if she intends to keep working as long as her mother. But her husband corrects her: "The answer, Kate, is that you don't really know. The kids and I have a bet that you'll be just like your mother."

Now What?

Having retired from community boards, I watch with admiration (and great pleasure) the "tech" generation find new and creative ways of dealing with the challenges of our fast-moving world. At the same time a nagging question keeps interrupting my new-found leisure time: "What now Kate? Are you ready and willing to live without a plan of action?" I recall in my high school year book a Latin phrase that always seemed applicable to me, *"She moves on with careful steps."* I wish Miss Simpson were around today to discuss some potential next steps.

The bottom line is not that there is a problem with keeping busy, but for me it has always been important to be useful or helpful in some way. Family, mentors and education have allowed me to become actively involved in whatever turned up. Now, in the ninth decade of my life, most people assume that both physical and metal capacities are diminishing and that it's my time to relax and enjoy family, friends and a strong genetic history.

Miss Simpson, Kate Webster's high school Latin teacher

There is no denying that I am enjoying a slower "pace" and the time it gives, to watch the garden on a daily basis, to read for an hour or two during the day, to revive the lost art of writing letters, and even just to sit and enjoy my peaceful surroundings. But there is still the urge to be involved. Bainbridge Island is a busy, caring, inclusive community and I'm confident the opportunities to contribute in some small fashion will turn up. As the Bible has said, "To everything there is a season and time to every purpose under heaven."

Patience has never been my strong suit but even a slow learner makes progress. Life has been extraordinarily good to me—a full complement of love and joy, happiness and a fair share of sadness and loss, but never have I been alone. Every step has been shared with family and dear friends.

Each of the communities we have lived in has added depth and meaning to my life, and now, at "Sunnybranch," with time to reflect and enjoy and—yes—relax, no one could ask for more.

Children's Hospital Foundation
2000
W. J. Pennington Award
is hereby presented to

Kate B. Webster

for distinguished and extraordinary commitment to
Children's Hospital and Regional Medical Center
as evidenced by leadership, dedication and service.

Scott D. Oki, Chairman
Children's Hospital Foundation
Board of Trustees

Sue Albrecht, Chairman
Children's Hospital & Regional Medical Center
Board of Trustees

Part IV

Anne Mae Seligman Belcher

July 6, 1895 – August 11, 1995

MEMORIALS SET FOR DR. BELCHER

We are sorry to report the death of Dr. Anne Belcher, mother of Kate Webster and grandmother of Kelly Scribner, just a few weeks after her 100th birthday.

Dr. Belcher was born in New York City in 1895, and spent her life practicing medicine as an ear, nose and throat specialist. She graduated medical school in 1922, at a time when women physicians were rare, and cared for generations of families during her 65 year medical career.

"She took care of everyone from celebrities to the people next door," said her daughter Susie. "She had great compassion, and she was a lady through and through. We all loved her very much."

Within the last couple of years, Dr. Belcher moved to Seattle to be closer to family, and has resided at Horizon House in Seattle where she had many friends. A memorial service will be held at Horizon House in Seattle on Monday, August 28, at 2 p.m.. A memorial is also scheduled for October 15 at the Cosmopolitan Club in New York City.

On Bainbridge Island, a celebration of Dr. Belcher's life is scheduled at the home of Kate Webster on Monday evening, August 28, at 7 p.m. All are welcome to attend. Address: 15369 Broom St. NE, Bainbridge Island.

Memorials may be made in Dr. Belcher's name to The Island School, Bainbridge Island, or to The Associates Fund, Horizon House, Seattle.

NY TIMES

BELCHER—Dr. Anne M., age 100. Physician in New York City for 68 years, died Friday, August 11, at her home in Seattle. Ear-Nose-Throat specialist to hundreds of New Yorkers and their families. Mother of Kate Webster of Bainbridge Island, WA, and Suzanne Platt Bunzel of Los Angeles, grandmother of six, and great-grandmother of seven; beloved by all. Memorial services will be held at a later date. Contributions may be sent to the Anne Belcher Endowment Fund, Cornell Medical School, 525 E. 68th St., NYC 10021.

NY TIMES - CORNELL

BELCHER—Dr. Anne M. The Boards, Faculty and Staff of The New York Hospital-Cornell Medical Center mourn the loss of our beloved colleague, Dr. Anne M. Belcher. A pioneering woman in her field, Dr. Belcher graduated from Cornell University Medical College in 1920 and joined the faculty in 1933. She will long be remembered as a devoted physician who maintained an active practice for more than 68 years and as an educator who taught generations of residents in our Department of Otorhinolaryngology. Our deepest condolences are extended to her family.

Sanford I. Weill, Chairman
Board of Overseers
Robert Michels, M.D., Dean
Cornell University Medical College
John F. McGillicuddy, Chairman
Board of Governors
David B. Skinner, M.D., President
The New York Hospital
W. Shain Schley, M.D., Chairman
Dept of Otorhinolaryngology

"Rest eternal grant her, O Lord, and let light perpetual shine upon her."

ANNE MAE BELCHER-1895 - 1995

Anne Mae Belcher, a name worthy of immortality. What better gesture of my love and respect then to name my work boat and run-about, my San Juan Islands transportation, after my grandmother.

Not a fancy boat, she's built stout, with very *tradition* lines, able to withstand confused seas, responding to each challenging wave with *determination and directness* as she carries her passengers safely along their route.

She is filled with sophisticated knowledge, in the navigation equipment on board. I am always guided by confidence that the data is exact, or *at least*, well informed.

All these qualities describe Anne Belcher, Nana, to most of us for all our lives. She was our guide, our counselor, our severest critic and strongest supporter. She will remain in our minds, the strong willed Matriarch of our family.

We will miss her very much.

CRAIG L. WEBSTER

Holt W. Webster
15369 Broom Street Northeast
Bainbridge Island, Washington 98110

We all know that in her two years as a Northwesterner, Mother had not become a total convert--98 years of East Coast living was deeply ingrained and could not quickly fade away.

But she did develop a deep appreciation for our Puget Sound country. She loved the mountains, our year-round gardens, and she even learned to walk in our Northwest mist--not always smiling, but she walked.

Most of all, Mother was amazed by the warm, welcoming, friendly people! Everywhere she was greeted, often by name, and more than anything else this made her feel she belonged.

Mom often didn't remember names, but her descriptions to me of those she met were unique. Our thanks to you all--you made a huge difference.

Mother had a long, full, productive life. She did what she wanted to do. You helped to round it out with your warm reception of her and your friendship.

We thank you all.

KATE WEBSTER

Kate On The Phone "With" Her Mother

ANNE M. BELCHER
Remembrance Service
Cosmopolitan Club
October 16, 1995

Kate Webster

I don't think I'll start my stories or we'll never get through. It has been wonderful hearing from all of you and getting another dimension. And although we have heard many of the stories, we certainly learned many new stories today!

One little addition to Mac Bundy's story. When Mother was visiting us in 1960 on Bainbridge Island, my husband was in the air freight business and he thought he could do anything in the airline world. And Mother said, "Well, I have to get to the White House tomorrow" and Holt said, "Well, I'll see what I can do." And about an hour later he said, "There isn't a seat anywhere on any plane, even in the cockpit." And Mother said, "Well that's too bad. I'll call and tell him I can't come," which she did. And an hour after that there was a call from the White House saying, "You're on 8 o'clock tomorrow morning."

I wanted to thank you all for coming today and for sharing your memories with us. I think perhaps the great-grandchildren learned more than anybody--and don't forget it! It has been an unforgettable occasion to come here, to gather old friends, and some people we have known about or heard about for many years and not met. Mother would have loved it. She would have pooh-poohed the whole idea and said, "Oh, you don't want to do that. You shouldn't be there." But she would have loved the reminiscences and she would have one-upsed all of us before we were through, I am sure.

Each of you, in your own way, held a unique spot in Mom's world. She cared about you and she certainly spent a lifetime caring about all her patients and all her friends. And I think all her patients did become friends.

As Suzie said, and we want you to be sure and understand this, she was sharp right until the time she decided that she had had it. And I am absolutely convinced she was in control and calling the shots. There is no question in my mind. My son and daughter-in-law and I had dinner with her and she said she was very tired so we tucked her into bed, kissed her good-night, and she went to sleep and never woke up. She did stay around long enough for Suzie to come up from L.A. and I am sure she knew that. I told her the next morning that Suzie was coming and she smiled and waited and then she departed in peace and we were with her.

We do also want you to know that because I think many of you care about this, that yesterday we had a family memorial service in New Jersey and we buried her there with Dad so she is back in the land that she loved so much.

We hope you will stay around awhile, talk with us and with each other, and share as many memories as you care to. Thanks so much.

126

The Seligman Story

In the first decades of our lives, my sister and I led protected, scheduled, predictable lives. We were surrounded by people we loved and trusted. We were well taken care of.

We lived in the Gramercy Park area of downtown New York City, and we played in the park every day. Weekends were spent with Mother and Dad, either in New York City or out in Far Hills, New Jersey, in the spring, summer, and fall. Some of Mother's and Dad's friends would come for dinner, and this was an opportunity to teach us manners, how to behave in front of grown-ups. We didn't know much about the real world.

When I was six years old, and Suzie four, Mother announced we were going to the seashore at Keyport, New Jersey, to spend a day with our grandparents. It was the first I had ever heard of Mother's family. Suzie and I were very aware of our Grandmother, and uncles, and cousins and aunts all gathered together in Far Hills. We never thought about having another family.

I never knew why, until many years later we were invited down there. Our grandparents, Russian-Jewish immigrants, had disowned Mother when she married Dad, a Christian. Mother had not heard from her mother and father since. Nor did my mom's brothers or sisters ever correspond with her.

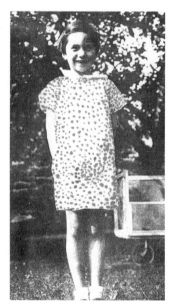

But that day we went down to the seashore, I remember having lunch in the kitchen with my grandmother, who prepared a salad lunch; everything was cold. And I remember my grandfather, who owned a successful "Mom And Pop Store"—with everything you can imagine in it! After we had lunch, Grandfather asked me if I would like to pick out a dress, which of course, at six years old, I was delighted to do. I can still picture that dress (see photo). It had little green apples all over it—not my colors at all!—but I thought it was a beautiful little dress, and I wore it for as long as it fit me.

We have pictures, also, of Mother and Dad with us on the beach. But we never did get any pictures of my grandparents.

Kate's Apple green Polka-dot Dress

To this day I don't know why we were invited, but I suspect my maternal grandparents wanted to meet their grandchildren. It was the only connection we had with the family for the rest of our lives with Mom. We had been disowned. It hurt. It hurt badly and forever. Mom and Dad had a Jewish wedding, at the insistence of my paternal grandparents, as well as an Episcopal church wedding. Mom's family attended the Jewish wedding, but none of them came to the other ceremony at Grace Church in Newark, New Jersey. My paternal grandparents attended both.

One of our family traditions growing up was that Mom and Dad, during the winter months, went to Newark to have dinner with Nana, Dad's mother. Nana was the matriarch of the Belcher family. It was a dedication on my parents' part, at which, as I grew older, I marveled, because Saturday evenings was their only free night off—it took real dedication to maintain this tradition, to stay in touch with that side of the family all those years.

When Suzie and I were little, we stayed home at the apartment with the housekeeper who paid little attention to us, staying in her own room. As we grew into our teenage years, we had the apartment to ourselves, and we explored every inch of it. I was the curious one, and I just wanted to find out what was hiding where. We spent time going through the big cedar chest in Mother's and Dad's room—full of their treasures. It was a lovely huge chest, which I still have. One day we explored to the bottom of the chest, and Suzie saw a Bible. She picked it up and found it was a Jewish Bible (the Tanakh), in Hebrew. There was no writing in it to indicate where it came from, and there was not a thought in our minds of connecting it with the family we had visited a decade before in Keyport, New Jersey.

Finally, in later teen years, Dad explained to us how Mother had been disowned by her family for marrying a Gentile, how her brothers and sisters had been raised never to contact her, and how much it hurt her. Mother carried this pain through the rest of her life. Dad told us this so affected her that she always hid her feelings as much as possible. It helped me understand why Mother seemed never to be demonstrative about anything. Apparently as a teenager and in college she was known as a party girl, full of fun. Now and then, one could still see that spark, but she hid it pretty successfully from most of the world.

Dad told us that Mother would bear the scars of this pain in relationships with her family for the rest of her life, that she didn't want us to ask her questions about her family, that she didn't want to talk about it, didn't want to think about it. Although I am sure it never was far from her mind, I truly believe her success was due as much to her intelligence, abilities and drive as to a desire to prove she was as good or better than anyone in her family. If she was not proud, she was certainly contented with what she achieved in her life, and she had many friends and family who thought highly of her and were proud of her.

For years my children have been curious about their grandparents and their families, and have at times been frustrated that there was not more information about their grandmother's side of the family.

In 2008, my daughter Anne Webster Fox decided to do a Google search of "Seligman," Mom's maiden name. The first article that appeared was an obituary in the New York Times in 2007 about Benjamin Seligman, a well-known New York lawyer, who had died at age 103. Anne called to ask if this person could have been my uncle. I believed that's who he was, so Anne wrote to the Rabbi of the Synagogue but never got a reply. The article mentioned Ben's wife, Florence, and daughters Stephanie and Nicole, both prominent attorneys in New York City. My sister, daughters and I were anxious to meet this unknown part of our family, but, not really knowing all the history, were hesitant to intrude in a manner that might still be painful or unwanted. We decided to try and find a third party to make the initial connection in order to leave the Seligmans free to refuse.

Scott Williams, Holt's godson, lived on the East Coast, did business in New York City, and had wide connections. He then did some research, discovering that one of his friends was a good friend of Nicole Seligman's husband, Joel Klein. Upon being contacted, the family indicated they would very much like to meet us. Apparently they knew about us, but thought we might be reluctant to make contact, given the family history.

Our first meeting was in the fall of 2009, with Suzie, Kelly, Annie, and me.

We have kept in touch and gotten to know the girls and Florence as friends. As the conversations back and forth have continued, we have enjoyed hearing about their lives. It turns out the extended Seligman family has never been close. Mother was the oldest of seven children, and Benjamin was the next youngest. The two boys, Benjamin and his younger brother, were both lawyers. Four of five girls were professionals, teachers, doctors, and they all led busy and productive lives. Grandfather Nathan Seligman, Mother's father, not only was owner of a successful mom-and-pop store, but invested wisely every penny he could spare in real estate, becoming a wealthy man of his generation. He thus was able to send all his children to college, and for Mother that included medical school. It was an amazing achievement for someone who jumped ship as an immigrant!

Apparently avoiding conscription into the German Army, Nathan Seligman reputedly landed in New York Harbor probably sometime in the late 1880s. No one seems to know how he ended up in Keyport, New Jersey, where he made friends with two brothers from Russia. At some point Nathan announced that he would like to get married, but had so far not found anyone suitable. The two brothers said they had a sixteen year old sister at home and would send for her. Sophia arrived alone from Riga, Latvia. My mother was born the next year. The rest is history.

Mother did tell us that her favorite sister Flora had died shortly after childbirth, and Flora's son Floyd had been brought up by her sister Bertha who never married. Lillian was the one relative who (after their parents died) would occasionally call and talk to Mother. I also believe mother financially assisted several of her sisters.

When I was visiting Mother in New York, just before her move to Seattle, she said Lillian had called; she was in the City and wanted to meet me. She came for tea, and we had a lovely chat. Lillian was not as vivacious as Mom, but she was bright and funny, and it was a treat to meet her.

Susie and I are both so very grateful to Annie for pursuing her desire to reconnect with our lost family and bring us all back together.

Dad, Sister Suzie, Kate

Mother, Sister Suzie, Kate

Dad with his violin at age 8.

Harold Stewart Belcher

6 October 1893 – 18 April 1988

Dad in Nassau, April 1941. It was Spring Break and my 17th Birthday. We stayed at the Royal Victorian Hotel. It was at dinner one evening that we saw the Duke and Duchess of Windsor.

Dad, c. 1940s—typical rainy day dress going off to work.

Dad was an unusual man for his time. Wife, children, mother, church, his dog, his patients—these were his life, what he really cared about. One other thing, he had a great love of classical music. Most Thursday nights during NY winters, he played his violin in a local quartet.

Every day WQXR, the classical NY station was on—it was the background to our life.

Dad made a chocolate cake every Saturday. On Thursdays our housekeeper was off, and Dad always cooked dinner. Mother said she'd done enough in the kitchen growing up. The only thing she ever cooked was meatloaf and fillet of sole—the latter which she believed was the best!

As I entered my teens, I began to realize that people felt very comfortable with Dad, that people confided in him and asked his advice. Dad was the silent one. On that trip to Nassau, in 1941 when I turned 17, people kept coming up to him and talking. I asked if he knew them. "No," he told me. "I think they just needed someone to talk to."

Dad and I loved to swim. Any beach, we would stay for hours swimming, while Mother and Suzie sat on the beach reading. Dad taught me to go with the water, flow with it, like body surfing.

As Dad got older, he and Mom would come to Bainbridge Island, and Dad just loved swimming in the bay—*at 55 degrees!*—just floating around for half an hour.

The 2000 Belcher Family Reunion

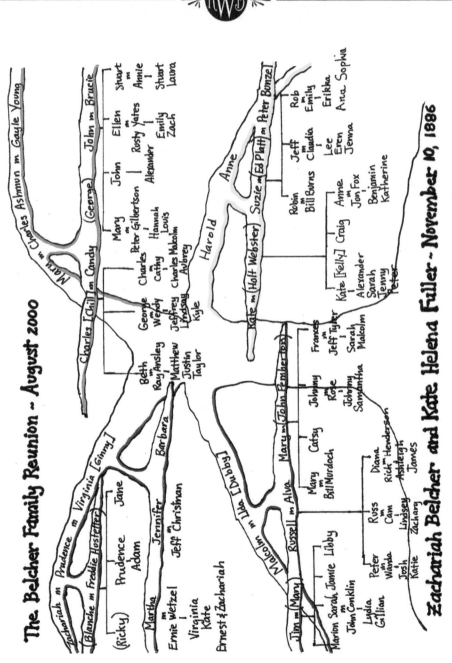

The Belcher Family Reunion ~ August 2000

Zachariah Belcher and Kate Helena Fuller ~ November 10, 1886

Recalling Geo Ashmun's idea in 1936 of a family reunion in the year 2000, the remaining cousins planned and enjoyed a grand four day weekend celebration.

Reunion 2000 – Smile!…

Jonathan, Russ, Peter, Cammie, Wanda, Rick, Bill M., Beth, Anne, Rob, Prue, Bill B., Craig, Jeff P., Jeff C.
Martha, Diana, Mary M., Jane, Barbara, Mary G., Robin, Kelly, Claudia, Jennifer

The Seniors: Mary P.(Mame), Russ, Kate, Chil, Johnny, Suzie

Back: Martha, Jennifer, Barbara   Front: Mame, Russ, Kate, Chil, John, Suzie

The Websters: Sarah, Jon, Craig, Alex
              Jenny, Anne, Kate, Kelly   Peter S., Kai, Ben, Katherine

Part V

The Story of Pacific Air Freight & Airborne Express

Summary Of Some Of Holt Webster's Post-Retirement Activities
Written By His Loving Wife At The Request Of A Group Of His Peers (Fall 1988)

The Pacific Air Freight sign has hung over our carport for many years

In the years before his retirement in 1984, Holt worked hard to help lead Airborne Freight Company move into the position of prominence in the airfreight world that it holds today. Although time was at a premium, Holt always recognized his responsibility as a community leader and contributed his time and talent as fully as he was able. He lead one of the early drives to develop support for the Corporate Council Of The Arts, maintained a continuing involvement in Rotary,  including community work, and was president of the Seattle Chamber of Commerce in 1980.

With retirement came more time to spend in his community. Holt made a decision to devote his energies in areas where his experience would be of the most use. On Bainbridge Island, Holt became a member of the Juvenile Diversion Program. This group met monthly to judge first offenses, mostly misdemeanors, of minors, to impress on them the implications of breaking the law and to hand out fitting penalties. Holt cared about these youngsters, and he had the ability to help them understand how important it was to start again. He was able to get across to these young offenders that they were being offered a once-in-a-lifetime chance to wipe the slate clean.

In the 1980s, public institutions of higher education in Washington state had begun intensive campaigns to raise private funds in order to enhance programs that were not adequately funded. Holt felt strongly that community colleges, an important part of the Higher Education system, did not have enough business support. So Holt joined the newly established Seattle Central Community College Foundation. For the past several years Holt led a program to develop annual commitments from the business community to this foundation. At the same time, he felt it important to educate Seattle leaders about the vital mission of this segment of our educational system. Holt devoted himself tirelessly to this task and has since been recognized by the State's community colleges with a service award.

Senior Services of Seattle was also seeking to expand its Board with members who would be able to educate a broader segment of the community on its needs. Holt became interested in the quality and variety of the program and joined the Board. He subsequently became a dedicated spokesman for Senior Services and has helped to bring other retired businesspeople on board, as well as lending his administrative skills to the agency.

Holt's Family: Uncle Jack, Grandmother Burns, Grandfather Burns (early 1930s)

Holt felt strongly that everyone should share personal success with his or her community in as many ways as possible. True to this belief, he has given advice and council to many young people starting out in business. He continued to sit down and talk through ideas and problems with aspiring entrepreneurs and his support and interest inspired those who sought him out.

1984—Holt Webster Retires From Airborne Freight Company

Airborne Key Dates
1946: Airborne Flower Traffic Association of California begins shipping exotics from Hawaii.
1951: Pacific Air Freight is founded in Seattle.
1968: Airborne and Pacific merge.
1980: Airborne buys Midwest Air Charter and Clinton County (Ohio) Air Force Base.

1983: National advertising campaign takes on Federal Express.

1999: U.S. Postal Service partnership brings Airborne into the residential delivery market.

(Source: http://www.fundinguniverse.com/company-histories/Airborne-Freight-Corporation-Company-History.html)

Portrait was surprise at Holt's retirement

A fine oil painting of Holt Webster now hangs at the end of the hallway on the fourth floor of the General Office.

The portrait was a surprise element in the festivities which honored Holt at his retirement.

The portrait measures 24 by 28 inches and it was painted by well-known Pacific Northwest artist, Ted Rand.

When Rand was commissioned to do the portrait, the decision was made to make it a surprise. That, of course, meant that the artist could not have formal "sittings" with his subject.

He did, however, need to have expo-sure to Holt so that he could portray him in a true fashion. At the January G.O. annual plan presentation, Rand did get the chance to observe Holt by pretending to be one of the Airborne employees attending.

While the meeting proceeded, he made mental notes of mannerisms and such. He then went back to his studio and with the assistance of several photographs, turned out the portrait.

The result is a remarkably fine representation of Holt Webster which now graces the General Office and which will hang in the new building as well. ✈

1951—Holt Webster joined Pacific Air Freight.

The Horatio Alger Story

Salesman, Pick-up, Delivery, etc.

1951 - 62

DR. HAROLD: DO YOU SUPPOSE OUR NEW
SON-IN-LAW IS KINKY?

DR. ANNE: I DON'T KNOW, BUT IT
SURE IS STRANGE ORDERING A CAR WITH-
OUT A BACK SEAT...

PacAir President 1962 - 1968

IN ELEVEN YEARS HE ROSE FROM THE
SECOND PERSON HIRED FULL-TIME TO
THE COMPANY PRESIDENCY

December 1968, Airborne Freight Corporation and Pacific Air Freight merged. Holt was president from 1968 to 1978, and Airborne Chairman of the board from 1978 to 1984.

AiRBORNE Today

AIRBORNE FREIGHT CORPORATION   VOL. 10, NO. 5   MAY 1978

Airborne looks to future with executive title changes

In a move designed to assure continued top-quality leadership of Airborne, the Board of Directors has approved title changes for the company's executive officers.

On April 24, Holt W. Webster was promoted from president to chairman of the board. He remains chief executive officer responsible for all Airborne activities.

Robert G. Brazier was promoted from executive vice president to president and retains the title of chief operating officer.

Robert S. Cline was promoted to vice chairman of the board, continuing as chief financial officer.

Mr. Webster explains that the title changes will not have a substantial, immediate effect but are, rather, the first step in a long-range plan.

"Obviously, change has to happen," he states. "I've been president and chief executive for 16 years. With Bob Cline and Bob Brazier in their respective jobs for many years, we've not had a lot of change. In six years, I'll be 65 and will definitely retire. It's time to set the wheels in motion for a smooth transition.

"During this time, Bob Brazier and Bob Cline will assume more and more responsibility which, in turn, will mean changes down the line as they delegate and reorganize. It should have a domino effect, opening up opportunities for others thoughout the company."

Another change approved by the Board was appointment of Accounting Director Jack Wilbourne to the position of corporate secretary. He had been assistant secretary since 1970.

Vern Williams, who was secretary for more than 25 years, becomes assistant secretary.

Chairman of the Board Holt W. Webster

President and Chief Operating Officer Robert G. Brazier

Vice Chairman and Chief Financial Officer Robert S. Cline

Kate who?

The man in the p.j.'s is Holt Webster, President of Airborne Freight Corporation and founding father of Airborne's new Complaint Department. And he and the five top Vice Presidents of the company have been getting calls at all hours.

It all started a couple of months ago when Airborne announced a revolutionary promise: If any Airborne customer had a serious problem, he was invited to call 800-426-0330 toll-free anytime of the day or night and give us hell.

You'll be glad to know it's working. We have had calls and every one of them has been handled by Air-

borne's top management, *personally*.

It's been a good lesson for us. We've discovered answers to a few problems we never knew existed. And that's really why we have a top management Complaint Department.

We have 1500 dedicated people in 64 key markets throughout the world. And we feel that our computer-linked communications system is the most efficient in the air-freight industry. But our system isn't perfect. Not yet. And if we really want to be the biggest in our industry, we simply have to be the best. Even if it means losing a little sleep.

Airborne
Give us the business.

Airborne's new
complaint department is
working out just fine.

Airborne Freight Corporation, Seattle, Washington 98104 / In Washington State call collect 206-623-7700

Watch out Federal . . .

Source: Air Cargo World, Communication Channels, Inc. ("cocking a snook at" is slang for "taking a look at")

International Report

More Scandal in the U.K.

There is never a dull moment in the British air forwarding industry. The latest scandal centers around Kuehne & Nagel Air Cargo Limited, its managing director, Ben Trinkler, and sales director, Anthony Hardy. Both men are being pressed to reveal their connection as directors with another forwarding concern trading under the improbable name of Red Baron Limited.

The existence of the Red Baron company came to light a year ago during an arms smuggling trial at London's Old Bailey Criminal Court when three well-known arms dealers were sent to prison for their part in smuggling arms to South Africa. During the course of the trial it was revealed that the forwarding company that handled the shipments was none other than Kuehne & Nagel, aided and abetted by the mysterious Red Baron. Since the trial, strenuous efforts have been made to conceal the fact that Red Baron ever existed, but recently its activities and those of Kuehne & Nagel in the arms smuggling business have attracted the attention of the authorities in Switzerland, where the latter company is registered. A full inquiry is currently under way there.

Meanwhile, in the U.K. the Institute of Freight Forwarders (IFF), of which Trinkler is a professional member, has been pressed to call upon him to explain his involvement in the Red Baron company, which describes him in its registration particulars as the managing director. Interestingly, Kuehne & Nagel Air Cargo is not a member of the British Forwarder's Institute. It resigned its membership in 1979 following a U.K. government inquiry into certain activities of the company's surface forwarding arm that resulted in criminal proceedings against some of its executives. Red Baron, likewise, is not a trading member of the Institute, nor does it hold accreditation from IATA.

Kuehne and Nagel seems to be plagued by investigations into its activities: shortly after the U.K. government's investigation, the company appeared before an investigation and public hearing ordered by the U.S. Federal Maritime Commission, and shortly thereafter a K&N vice president was charged in the Canadian courts with being a party to kickback charges leveled against the president of Atomic Energy of Canada Ltd.

Ironically—or maybe not—in the face of his possible expulsion from the U.K. Forwarder's Institute, Trinkler recently announced record figures for the company during the first half of 1983. K&N Air Cargo exported 3,185,100 kilos of freight—almost as much as was lifted in the whole of 1982—and an increase of 86.6 percent over the same period of the previous year.

Airborne To Expand

Holt Webster, chairman and chief executive officer of Airborne Freight Corporation, made a whistle-stop visit to the U.K. on his way home to Seattle from a similar stop in Tokyo to preach the gospel of international expansion for Airborne.

The larger part of the corporation's resources, Webster said, will be invested in the international field. In fact, cocking a snook at Federal Express's long-avowed intention to begin service to Europe, Webster said Airborne is initiating west-bound service to complement its two-year-old east-bound service. Airborne's International Ex-Pack will use Frankfurt and London as the main hubs, providing overnight service to New York with guaranteed delivery before noon.

Webster believes Airborne is poised to launch its own corporate image in countries outside the U.S., starting in Europe. Prior to Webster's trip, trucks bearing the Airborne name and logo already had taken to the road in Europe, and Airborne had appointed its own operations people with its new agents in Holland and Belgium since the break with HAT Express. In both these countries Airborne appointed Damco Air as its exclusive agents, and in France it is using SET—one of the largest agents in the country.

Webster disclosed that he will retire from active participation in the air freight industry next April. He also reported that Airborne's claim against the Rotterdam-based Pak-

Holt Webster

hoed Group, arising from the termination of the reciprocal handling agreement between Airborne and the former HAT Express companies, has now been settled by mutual agreement.

Colin Mitchell

Mitchell Back in Circulation

British Airways' former cargo general manager, Colin Mitchell, who was a victim of the shakeup in the airline's new management structure, has returned to the air cargo industry as a forwarder. Mitchell has joined United Transport Limited, a vast conglomerate that itself is a wholly owned subsidiary of British Electric Traction (BET), which has a finger in many pies.

Mitchell, who holds director status, has been hired, initially, to coordinate the various air and surface forwarding operations of United. One of these with a distinct air freight flavor is Hill and Delamain, which is still recovering from massive losses it incurred in backing an all-cargo charter operator. H&D

One of Holt's *Investco* gang.

R. DUKE WATSON
BOX 70628
SEATTLE, WASHINGTON 98107

April 3, 1984

Dear Holt:

Through fate and/or circumstance we have been involved mutually over the years in a variety of activities. To enumerate a few:

1. digging garbage pits at Snoqualmie Pass;

2. swapping mattresses on front porches;

3. guzzling and dialectics with the "D and D gang";

4. East Newton-Federal neighborhood ruckuses;

5. Investco meetings beyond count.

A lot of good memories there. Along with all of these, another which stands out signifigantly for me, both sentimentally and practically, is my participation as an initial private offering subscriber in Airborne. I take this opportunity to express both my appreciation for having been a selected participant, and my pride in your achievements and those of the company you created.

May you and Kate enjoy to the full now, and during many delightful years to come, the fruits of your efforts. And perhaps we can get back eventually to the serious business of mattress swapping.

Sincerely, and with all best wishes,

Duke Watson

Mr. Holt Webster
Airborne Freight Corporation
P. O. Box 662
Seattle, Wash. 98111

And from one of Holt's more curious associates:

From the World Famous

Ye Olde Curiosity Shop, Inc.

"Beats the Dickens" — Most Unique Shop in the World
INDIAN TRADERS, IMPORTERS AND CURIO COLLECTORS
MUSEUMS SUPPLIED — MAIL ORDERS FILLED

601 ALASKAN WAY · PIER 51
SEATTLE, WASHINGTON 98104, U.S.A.
TELEPHONE (206) 682 - 5844

JOSEPH R. JAMES
PRESIDENT

Established 1899

March 29, 1984

Mr. Holt W. Webster
15369 Broom Street N.E.
Bainbridge Island, WA 98110

Dear Holt:

You are to be congratulated for good judgment in
retiring. The employees will be grateful, the Board will
finally be relieved, and the Corporation will undoubtedly
prosper. Fortunately, Kate's activities will keep her out
of the house, which should be a help to her morale--looks
good all the way around.

Best of luck on this new era in your life and may
your health permit you to live happily for many years to
come.

Yours sincerely,

Joe James

JRJ:cl

Enclosure

A long tome on a long affiliation:

LAW OFFICES

RIDDELL, WILLIAMS, BULLITT & WALKINSHAW

4400 SEATTLE-FIRST NATIONAL BANK BUILDING
SEATTLE, WASHINGTON 98154

(206) 624-3600

TELEX RCA 296338
RWBW UR

RICHARD H. RIDDELL
J. VERNON WILLIAMS
STIMSON BULLITT
WALTER WALKINSHAW
STEPHEN E. DEFOREST
DOUGLASS A. RAFF
VINCENT R. LARSON
DAVID D. HOFF
GEORGE E. FRASIER
NYLE G. BARNES
ROBERT J. BRYAN
LYN TANGEN
W. MICHAEL HAFFERTY
JOHN D. LOWERY
GORDON W. WILCOX
BRUCE T. BJERKE

OF COUNSEL
SNYDER J. KING

DAVID D. BUCK
DONALD M. CURRIE
JOSEPH E. SHICKICH, JR.
PATRICK D. McVEY
THOMAS W. BURT
DANIEL S. GOTTLIEB
MAUDE ANDERSON
HUGH R. TOBIN
NANCY E. KENNEDY
THOMAS G. HAMERLINCK
CRAIG M. LAWSON
LORRIE D. NORTHEY
ALISON MOSS
KYLE R. SAMUELS
RODNEY L. BROWN, JR.
HARRY E. GRANT, JR.
GERALD KOBLENTZ
KEITH A. BUCHHOLZ

April 3, 1984

Mr. Holt W. Webster
Airborne Freight Corporation
190 Queen Anne Avenue North
P.O. Box 662
Seattle, Washington 98111

Dear Holt:

It now seems clear that this time you really intend to retire in that you have assured the event by going public with it and insisting that the Board name your successor.

While I understand and am sympathetic with the occurrence, it nonetheless evokes a flood of emotion and recollection of nostalgic events over the past thirty plus years, which focus on the question whether the man and the company are really separable.

As this letter may be viewed by other than your own eyes, I'll spare you the emotion, but the following remembered circumstances and events (assisted in part by rummaging some old files) may have bearing.

Your company of course started before you by Gruger Robinson and Mann in October, 1949, with total paid-in capital of $6,000, half of which was represented by the assets of Ocean Shipping Company of Tacoma, being hard assets of $500 and goodwill of $2,500.

You apparently bought a job with the company in November, 1950, subscribing for 30 shares, and then another 20 in the following February. By August of 1951, you were there for good and were elected Vice President. The shareholders' meeting on that day instructed "that the Board of Directors make every effort to develop new sources of revenue and take advantage of any opportunity presented to keep the company in operation and report to the shareholders again in October." Still a mighty perilous existence.

Mr. Holt W. Webster
April 3, 1984
Page 2

You may remember that in April, 1952, existing deficits were squeezed out of corporate capital by reducing par value of the stock on a ratio of one to four, it being noted that at that time the company had to withdraw from the domestic forwarding field and operate as an agent only.

From and after August, 1952, I can personally verify the chronicle of events as I became a member of the Board at that time. The company was indeed in a precarious position at that time, the minutes reflecting that the life of the company may depend on its success in negotiating a substantial discount on its indebtedness to the Flying Tiger line. It got even worse the next month when about half of the company's perishable air freight business to Alaska was lost to the new surface carrier, Ocean Van Line. A statement of policy was hammered out and formally adopted emphasizing both agency and forwarding to Alaska (which at that time required an international letter of registration) with the long-range objective of the company to re-enter domestic forwarding "to be pursued cautiously but with determination."

It is my personal recollection that during this early period, one of the duties of the Vice President was to pick up and deliver freight in his own car (the company didn't own a truck), and that normal working days spanned at least 14 hours.

Late in 1952 a tie-in was made with Norm Shaw in Anchorage, and Pacific Forwarding Corporation was authorized.

By June of 1953, things were picking up. The CAB authorization as an international forwarder was approved and the CAB approved interlocking control relationship between Pacific Air Freight and Pacific Forwarding. The financials in September, 1953, noted that the net worth of the company was only a negative $353.

You will remember the brief affiliation with George Dart, formerly of Flying Tigers-Slick, in the summer of 1954, and then the decision to close the New York office at the end of the year.

You will no doubt also remember that during this entire period, you not only personally guaranteed the company's bank loans, but even made direct loans to the company as well. Talk about betting the company! You bet the family!

Things looked up a little in 1955 when the company earned approximately $9,000. Things were even better by the end of

Mr. Holt W. Webster
April 3, 1984
Page 3

1956 when your lawyer's retainer was fixed at $75 per month. This period was salted and peppered by merger negotiations with Ace Air Freight, Midwest Delivery Service, the adding of names like Al Newman, Frank Gallagher, John Holahan, Joe Hackett in New York and Glenn Hodson in Portland.

In 1961, Sandell left the Board and you acquired Ed Hanby's Wings and Truck Transportation Company of Anchorage, and also initiated discussions with Frank Fernandez in Los Angeles. This culminated in a contract with Mark IV Messenger and Frank in early 1962. Your salary was fixed at $850 per month in April, 1962. Money was obviously still mighty tight as reflected by the Board in discussing a publicity brochure presented to it ruled that "The basic charge of $500 and a continuing monthly charge of $200 was deemed excessive for the type of proposal submitted." In November of that year, Gruger resigned as President and CEO and you were elected to succeed, in the face of the first net loss for the company in five years. The following January you stepped up again and loaned the company $17,000 for 90 days. You then considered alternatives of making deals with Mark IV, merging with Wings and Wheels, or merging with Airborne-California or with Smythe, and proceeded to negotiate agreements with Fernandez and with Aero Expediters, Inc., of New York (Gilbert Brean). During the following year, consideration was given to merger with Four A Air Freight Forwarding, Red Bird Delivery and AEI.

Bob Brazier, late of Aero Expediters, became Vice President of Sales in April, 1965, and the following month the agreement with the Breens was terminated. The first reference to Bob Cline as administrative assistant to the President appears in the July, 1965 minutes. At that time, Fernandez resigned as a director, to be replaced by Larry Rodberg, who brought Nicolette and Leong into the company as well. In August, 1965, Cline was elected Vice President of Finance, Treasurer and Assistant Secretary, and the minutes noted that you were still guaranteeing the company's borrowings at Sea-First. That fall, Touche Ross Bailey & Smart were appointed as auditors to the company and at your suggestion, all executive bonuses were foregone in the interest of preserving working capital needed for the growth of the company. Several Board meetings were livened by confrontations with Gil Breen, including a visitation by the U.S. Marshal. The ups during this period were the appearance of Faulkner, Dawkins & Sullivan to assist in financing. The downs included the airline strike in summer of 1966, resulting in severe personnel cutbacks and even suspension of director's fees. In October of 1966, Brazier joined the Board after Terry Thompson's resignation, and the following

Mr. Holt W. Webster
April 3, 1984
Page 4

January Cline also joined to fill a vacancy from Hugh Smith's resignation.

You may also have some remembrance of the CAB enforcement proceedings, including the complaint filed by Airborne-California in early 1967 with questionable motivation and bona fides. Notwithstanding this, an agreement for merger with Airborne-California was hammered out (the term used advisedly) the following year, and ultimately approved by the Justice Department and the CAB on the failing company doctrine. Just how failing did not become clear until the year-end audit following the merger.

The following year you unified the Board behind you and your team and it has been a success story ever since.

The company bears your stamp and your character. You will be ably followed, but never replaced.

With this letter goes my personal thanks for the privilege of working with you during these years, and best wishes for enjoyment and satisfaction in what lies ahead.

Sincerely,

J. Vernon Williams

258L:JVW/jm
4/3/84

April 2, 1984

Mr. Holt Webster, Chairman
Airborne Freight Corporation
190 Queen Anne Ave. North
Seattle, WA 98111

I don't understand, Holt,

why you're hanging it up so soon.

Thirty-three years with the same outfit is only about
8712 working days. Or, at ten hours a day, 87,120 hours
of doing pretty much the same stuff.

Boy, you sure get bored quick!

Here's wishing you 33 happy years as Bainbridge Island's
premiere gardener.

Regards,

Don

Donald B. Kraft
President

DBK:ja

And from the competition, a gracious letter of kind regards.

John C. Emery, Jr.
Chairman and
Chief Executive Officer

Executive Offices
Wilton, Connecticut 06897
203 834-3321

April 17, 1984

Mr. Holt W. Webster, Chairman
Airborne Freight Corporation
19 Queen Anne Avenue, N
P.O. Box 662
Seattle, WA 98111

Dear Holt:

I couldn't let the occasion of your impending retirement go by
without saying how much I'll miss you at industry affairs and other such times
our paths have crossed in the past. As a believer in the principle "people
buy people first, and companies second," you have personified the best in your
representation as Airborne's Chief Executive Officer, and I salute you on your
most successful career in air cargo as well as compliment you for the
exemplary way you have acted as one of Emery's worthy adversaries.

We are a better industry because of your presence and the many
contributions you have made towards the overall reputation and integrity for
which the air freight forwarding industry is now known. Your innovative
ideas, combined with an outstanding senior management group, like the two
Bob's, have helped catapult Airborne into a real leadership position in air
freight for which you can take great pride.

I wish it were possible for me to be with you at the dinner
celebrating your 33 years of service to your company and its predecessor, but
hope this letter from a good friend of yours will do the honors for me until I
see you the next time.

With congratulations on your over three decades of service to our
favorite vocation and best wishes on this next new phase of your life.

With kind personal regards.

Cordially,

John C. Emery, Jr.

JCEjr/mal

156

And the humor, there was always humor.

Be it known by these presents
that the gold medal award

ATHLETE
OF THE YEAR

has been won by

Holt W. Webster

He has amassed an astonishing
1492 points out of 1500 possible in the
decathlon, surpassing all others
in winning the following ten events:

(1) Jumping to conclusions,
(2) Pushing his luck,
(3) Wrestling with his conscience,
(4) Running down the competition,
(5) Pressing for an answer,
(6) Driving home a point,
(7) Bending over backwards,
(8) Squeezing out the truth,
(9) Scraping through the day, and
(10) Dragging bottom

Chief Judge

Walter T. McGovern

From the Diet:

LEWIS H. JOHNSON
P.O. Box 284
Medina, Washington 98039

April 12, 1984

Mr. Holt Webster
15369 Broom St. NE,
Bainbridge Island, WA 98110

Dear Holt:

I know I wasn't alone in enjoying your speech to the Diet Tuesday night, but I doubt that anyone in the audience enjoyed it more. God how I shared your struggles - the early years of no money, little or no expertise, creditors howling and friends despairing over your choice of occupation. Middle years with not enough money, incompetent and crooked employees, blood baths and merger talk. And the last years when unbelievably the thing turned around and a bunch of decisions in the past culminated in results beyond your dreams. From time to time I thought you were talking about my company, my career, not yours!! One major difference - I wrote no "state of the company" memo's to my staff. They wouldn't have read them anyway.

I hope the other members appreciated that your speech was excellent because in your casual off-hand way you were reliving in thirty minutes an intense business career that spanned 23 years. You can now face Kate and tell her that all the struggle, all the missed social occasions in the early years) was really worth it - - at least that's what I remind Sonia from time to time.

Good luck on your next career.

Sincerely,

Recollections Of Holt

Finally, some of the many recollections of Holt from friends and family are that he could be funny and he could be rude. He was often totally supportive, but sometimes he'd say you'd have to figure that out for yourself.

He believed in helping those in need, but always made sure there was a need. He was a demanding boss and exec., but was respected as an honest, caring, and available CEO.

One of my favorite recollections is a question from his younger daughter, when she was around 12 years old. "Mom. How do you know whether dad is joking or serious?" My answer, pretty much off the top of my head—but it still stands today—was, "I always assume he is joking. And when he isn't, I find out about it."

In earlier chapters I have included some of the episodes in Holt's life that were important, for our time, and for our family, and some of the episodes that were merely amusing. All add up to the person he was. But he was also my beloved husband, and I would like to share some of my favorite memories of our life together.

I first met Holt at my roommate Candy's wedding in Portland, Oregon. It was just after World War II. She married one of my first cousins, Charlie Ashman. I had traveled to Portland to be in the wedding, never having been west of Philadelphia, so it was quite an adventure for me. I was there a couple months before the wedding, and therefore I got to go camping and hiking around the northwest. I visited the Pacific Ocean, and it was a whole new world to me, and with which I immediately fell in love.

The night of the wedding there was a great big party at Candy's family, the McKee's house. I discovered that my sister and I thought we were going out with the same young man—not knowing quite how that happened. But I decided I was not interested, so, having been invited to stay in the family home, I headed upstairs to bed. Passing the front door, heading to the staircase, Holt Webster walked into the house. I did something I'd never done before, not knowing what prompted me, I changed my mind right there and then and decided I wanted to go to the party after all. I ran up to him, said, "Oh, there you are, I'd been looking all over for you. You've come back to enjoy the party!" He replied, "You bet. Let's go."

With that, Holt and I spent the rest of the evening together. And we stayed up talking to almost three in the morning—most everyone else having gone to bed—and we had discovered that we agreed on many basic issues.

The next day Holt was to head back to Seattle, to his job with Northwest Airlines. The following day my aunt and three cousins would be in Seattle, en route on a trip to a ranch in Calgary, British Columbia.

On the way home from the party, Holt asked me if he could take me out that following evening, in Seattle. I dutifully asked my Aunt Mary whether that would be alright—though I was 21 years old. In those days that was the proper thing to do. She liked Holt and said that would be just fine. "But," she added, "I would like you two to have dinner with us before you go out for the evening."

Holt arrived at the Olympic Hotel, where we were staying, to join Aunt Mary and me for dinner—my three cousins were dining with us also. We had reservations for the Georgian Room. It was a wonderful way to start what I didn't know was to be the rest of my life in Seattle.

That was our second date.

After that, we went back to the East Coast. I spent time with my family and made preparations to move to San Francisco to look for a job and do something about the rest of my life.

Engagement

I arrived in San Francisco in late November of 1946 and found a job with Crown Zellerbach, one of the largest paper companies in the world, which in 1928 started the famous paper mill in Port Townsend, Washington. It was a wonderful four-month experience for me, right out of College. I joined their training program and started work filing manila folders in a room that was probably ten-by-ten. The cramped space was full of these folders, having not been touched since before the war, and for some strange reason I really enjoyed the job (in fact I still like doing filing to this day). But I never found out what they were training me for, because, at the end of four months, I left to go back east to get ready to marry Holt Webster.

Before heading back east, on New Years of that year, I'd been invited to Portland to attend another wedding, this time of the sister of my roommate. Holt was going to be in the wedding, too; there were rumors about Holt and me among some of the mothers planning the wedding, and I think that is why they wanted us to attend. So I enjoyed four wonderful days in Portland—Holt and I were together constantly!

After the wedding, I went back to San Francisco. On Friday the 14th of February 1947, just coincidentally it being Valentine's Day and Holt having that day off, Holt came down to San Francisco for the weekend, and we got engaged. We called my mother and father to tell them the news. They were not totally surprised—for some reason. They didn't argue. They didn't say, "Do you know what you're doing?" The just said, "That's wonderful!" And they asked that we keep them posted. We told them we wanted to be married at the end of May and that I would be coming home fairly soon. They told me that was fine, and they would learn more when I got back to New York.

After hanging up the phone, Holt and I looked at each other and we said, "Do we really know what we're doing?" We decided that perhaps we should spend a little *steady time* together, to make sure we did. So Holt took a week of his vacation from Northwest Airlines and he and I went down to the Webster's beach cottage in Gerhardt, Oregon. Holt's father, Mr. Webster as I always called him, came with us to be our chaperone; that's the way we did it in those days. We spent a rainy March week, cold, wet, *blowey*, and absolutely wonderful. We walked along the beach and sat by the fire, played "Pounce," and we were thoroughly spoiled because Holt's father did all the cooking. And we talked and talked and talked, and we decided that we knew exactly what we were doing—for better or for worse.

With that settled, I went home back to New York, the end of March.

We were married the end of May, on the 27th, 1947.

Wedding And Honeymoon

One particular recollection of just how tolerant and understanding my parents were with all this news: The night Holt was to arrive from Seattle, traveling on a pass with Northwest Airlines, four days before we were to be married. Holt's parents drove across the country to New York. We were all to meet at Mom and Dad's apartment for dinner. The senior Websters arrived, and we were sitting there around the table. About 6:30 the phone rang, and it was Holt. He was calling from Detroit where he had been bounced, and he said "I'll get there as soon as I can." Amazingly enough, he arrived about a quarter of 9:00 PM, which was pretty good timing in those days. Meanwhile my mother and father and Mr. and Mrs. Webster spent those few hours really getting to know each other. Though things were a bit tense for a few minutes after Holt's phone call, everybody had a good sense of humor, and it all worked out just beautifully. I'd have to admit I was a bit of a nervous wreck, and I was very glad to see Holt when he arrived.

After a three-day honeymoon in the Poconos—we only had three days because Holt had used up both of his vacations that week in March we'd gone to Gerhardt, to the beach—we flew back to Seattle, to our first home, the bottom floor of an old house on Capitol Hill, right across from Volunteer Park. In mid-1947 there was not much to rent, and Holt had spent weeks trying to find an appropriate place for us. We had the bottom floor of the house, the living room, the dining room, kitchen, and shared the one upstairs bathroom with two other couples who both worked and each had one upstairs bedroom. There was a full basement, we all shared the laundry room, as well as a very pretty, little backyard, which was wonderful for me, as I was the only one not working at the time. It was an interesting start to a marriage.

Neither one of us had any friends in Seattle. In those days, Holt was working shifts at Northwest Airlines, and the weeks after we settled in to our new home Holt was working the graveyard shift. It was a very interesting start to married life. And the good part of it was, that not knowing anybody around us, not having any relatives in the area telling us anything that we "were supposed to be doing," we were totally reliant on each other, and we really got to know each other in ways that might not have been possible had we been surround by caring family.

Life Together

Three and a half years later, end of summer 1950, our daughter Kelly was two and a half, and Craig was six months old, and we had moved to our first little house on the corner of Newton Street and Federal Avenue. It was at this time Holt told me that he did not feel his future lay with Northwest Airlines. He and a friend, Phillip Gruger, had been discussing starting a business in airfreight. In those early years of our life together we had no money to spare and were just scraping along. But Holt's grandfather had bequeathed a small inheritance, and Holt said that if I agreed with his investing that money into the business, then he and Phillip would start it. This plan made sense to me. I came from a family of entrepreneurs, and I could understand his wanting to set out on this venture. And, so, Pacific Air Freight was started in January of 1951.

Right at the start of working for his new company, Holt sat me down—as he enjoyed doing from time to time—and said that he wanted to tell me that this was going to be a whole new way of living, it was going to be difficult, we were going to have to really watch our pennies, and I would have all the responsibility for running the household, paying the bills, taking care of the children. He said, "And that is your job." In those words, adding that he wanted very much to be a part of our lives, but it would only be as in the background for a while; and pretty much for the rest of his working life, that's the way it was.

It worked out well, this life of ours. Holt and I did communicate completely with each other. I knew what I was doing, and I enjoyed our life together. After Annie was born, and when the kids all started school, I had more time to branch out into the community to start my own career in volunteer work.

One of the most wonderful things about Holt, and about our relationship, was that we did share everything. We were completely honest with one another. Holt never kept anything from me, the good, the bad, the indifferent, what he thought, what he liked, what he didn't. It was all part of our life together, and it meant a great deal to me.

The stories of Pacific Air Freight and Airborne history, along with the memorials from our three children and various friends, give a wonderful picture of what Holt Webster was like.

Holt loved life. He loved his family. He loved his work. He loved Sunnybranch. And he lived every moment to the fullest. Even if it was just sitting down and looking out over the water.

Holt made his life plans and followed them more meticulously than anyone else I've ever known.

Coming to Seattle as bride and groom, the friends we met over the years always considered us a couple, and indeed we enjoyed our lives together—even as we enjoyed our ever-growing circle of friends. However, having had 22 years of life before meeting Holt, and there's no question in my mind that the day I met him in Portland, Oregon, September 2nd, 1946, on that day my life changed in many ways, my life changed forever.

My beloved Belcher family, whom I loved dearly, were not a "chatty" group. Yet, conversation was constant, and we all enjoyed each other. Nonetheless, I cannot remember many occasions, in my immediate family with Mom and Dad or in Far Hills where there was a huge amount of laughter or a lightheartedness.

Correspondingly, growing up, I was always serious, always frowning, taking everything seriously. I didn't know what I was missing. I was, one might say, not full of fun. I thought I was having fun. But looking back on it, my life was very composed, focused and organized.

Meeting Holt, who was a few years older, he did not at first seem my kind of guy. His reputation was that of a "party boy"—a Portland, Oregon, party guy, but clearly not a New York sort, and that was all right with me. He teased me from the first minute we met. And he made me laugh!

For much of our social life together, I was Holt's *straight person*. Some of our friends couldn't understand how I just stood there and took it, but it was all a big joke. Holt knew it, and he knew I knew it, and that was his style, and it was all right with me.

Even when we were alone, occasionally, he would talk to me about something, and I would suddenly realize that he was dead serious, and it was then going to be an important discussion.

One family story I remember well: Holt was an extremely generous person in so many ways, giving to his community, to his family, and to me. He never failed from our first Christmas on to surprising me most of the time with a present that I had really wanted and likely had talked about to the point that I stopped and it would slip my mind. And, come Christmas, there it would be! Our first Christmas, I had been thinking of a particular pair of shoes for a long time, then finally forgot about them; that Christmas, there they were all wrapped up under the Christmas tree.

Another Christmas some years later—I had been wearing my college bathrobe since we were married—there under the tree was a wonderful quilted, dark green robe from Eddy Bauer (which I am still wearing).

One Christmas, having been really sick for the first time in our marriage and in the hospital for a few days before Christmas, a little box lay under the tree. I was astounded! It held a beautiful diamond ring. I had talked for years about not having a diamond ring. Holt was delighted. And I treasure that ring to this day.

For years Holt had wanted to move to Bainbridge Island from Capitol Hill. We enjoyed Bainbridge Island so much in the spring and summer, and really through Thanksgiving. But I felt that having three teenagers in high school all at the same time would mean that I would be an island carpool mother, and that I would no longer have the time for the volunteer work which I loved in Seattle. Therefore, I suggested we wait to move to Bainbridge until all three kids had graduated from high school.

The day Annie, our youngest, was accepted to college, Holt said, "Well, okay, you've had your way for over twenty years, and now it's my turn." I dragged my feet a little bit, saying, "Well, I don't know whether I'm really ready for this move." Holt asked, "What would it take?" I hadn't even thought about it. I suppose I was being a little difficult and not willing to give in immediately. But Holt insisted, "I want to know what it would take?" Without even thinking, right off the top of my head, I said, "An indoor swimming pool." My thought was, swimming was good for me and I loved to swim, while Holt didn't care two hoots about swimming—and I guess I figured it would be far too much for him to even think about. He said immediately, "Okay, let's find an architect and get going."

That's how it went. We've been here 40 years, and there's no way I'd ever want to leave this beautiful property and home, which we all have loved and lived in so completely.

Plans And Dreams

From the time we met, Holt and I shared our thought and our plans and our dreams. When something was bothering one of us, the other always seemed to know. Sometimes it took a while to get the discussion going, but we always did manage to talk things through. When we didn't agree on something, we just kept talking until we did agree. About many things Holt was actually right more often than I. But at times I had my way.

Holt was always extraordinarily supportive of all the things in which I was involved, always helpful and encouraging in my volunteer work. And he shared his work with me—the problems, and the people, the plans and the dreams—the ups and the downs, and there were many, particularly in the early days. It was wonderful to feel a total involvement in what he was doing; and I think he felt the same way about my activities.

In 1984, when Holt retired, Airborne sent us on a fabulous, red-carpet trip around the world visiting each of the Airborne stations: [list the stations & countries visited?]. It was really wonderful. I met all the people at the various station, and we were also able to get out into the surrounding countryside wherever we visited. One of the highlights was four or five days with his German agent out of Frankfurt. She drove us through the Romantische Strasse (Romantic Road), 350 kilometers of highway winding through local towns and castles—including the famous Neuschwanstein castle—between Würzburg and Füssen in southern Germany, specifically in Bavaria and Baden-Württemberg. One of the delightful treats for me was that every time I saw one of the brown tour signs along the way I would say, "Oh, stop! Stop!" and that is what we did! On all our other trips together we just didn't have time to do that kind of thing. And so it was a tremendous treat. I remember even the Creglingen Fingerhutmuseum (the Thimble Museum in Creglingen) which we found in the Black Forest. Holt's response, "Oh, thimbles." But it had a fascinating history, with thousands of thimbles, and even he had to laugh at times before we got through.

It was an extraordinary trip, and we both enjoyed it tremendously. Afterwards, we came back to Bainbridge Island, and Holt settled in to the retired life, doing what he always dreamed about doing: puttering in the garden, playing a little golf, hitting a few tennis balls now and then, and come 5:00 in the afternoon, sitting on the deck with a Martini and just glancing out across the water in perfect peace—his favorite time of the day.

Holt died too young—and much too soon. But he did have eight good years of retirement at his beloved Sunnybranch. For this I am grateful. Our 45 years minus one month were an extraordinarily full, fun, happy, and often unpredictable life together. Having gotten married after only six dates, it does seem incredible that it all worked out so well—for which I am forever grateful. And the memories live on.

Now and then I can still hear him talking to me, often saying, "What in the Devil are you doing that for?" But then, always at night, I remember that he never went to sleep without saying, "I love you."

"I love you"—and hearing this is certainly one of the things I miss the most.

Part VI

Holt Wilson Webster & Craig Lewis Webster

"Holt Webster Of Airborne Express, An Executive Of Ability And Heart."
By Polly Lane, Seattle Times staff reporter[1]

"Holt Webster was a Seattle contributor in a big way. With little fuss or fanfare he helped the community in several ways.

"He built his company, Airborne Express, into the small-package big-leagues. He led a variety of civic groups, from the Greater Seattle Chamber of Commerce to the board of Senior Services of Seattle and King County. He sat on boards of directors of prominent business institutions.

"At the same time, the former chairman and chief executive officer of Airborne Express was competent, thoughtful and easy to work with, said his friends.

"Mr. Webster, who lived on Bainbridge Island, died Monday in a Bremerton hospital after a short illness. He was 72."

Holt Wilson Webster
June 15, 1919–April 15, 1992

---

1   (Wednesday, April 15, 1992 - Page updated at 12:00 AM) Copyright © 1992 Seattle Times Company.
http://community.seattletimes.nwsource.com/archive/?date=19920415&slug=1486549

April 18, 1992

Dear Dad,

I can't believe this.

Though you've spent years telling me you'd already lived longer than you expected or intended, and though my head has always known that no one goes on forever, my heart felt you were different. "Holt seemed indestructible." Dad, you've left us too soon. I still need you.

It wasn't always thus. Growing through the turbulent, testing years of adolescence challenged us both. I often felt your "opinion" didn't leave much room for mine; we didn't spend a lot of time on the same side of the fence! But we made it, Dad! And as I view it with the perspective of my 43 years, we did pretty darn well. You've been one of my best friends for years now.

I'm really going to miss you Dad. You believed in me. You believed in all of us, and because of that buoyant belief, and because you worked hard and honestly at everything you did, you inspired us to do our best, to stretch and to shine.

The people who love you span four generations. You liked being with us and we felt it. You were fun, you were funny. You were as easy and comfortable with my children's friends as you were with your own, and you made everyone around you feel comfortable and relaxed as well.

Your expectations were high, for yourself and for others. You were generous, you were forgiving, you were the least selfish person I know. You believed we all need to look out for each other and that we need to leave the world a better place than we found it. You did leave it a better place, Dad. Through your own efforts, you made many many lives richer. With your inspiration, we'll try to carry on. We'll try to do you proud. But we'll miss you.

I really want you back. There's so much more I wanted to share with you, to say, to do. Thank you, Dad, for all you gave to me, to my children, to my friends. I miss you terribly already. I'll love you always.

Kelly

HOLT WILSON WEBSTER - A GOODBYE FROM ANNIE

DAD YOU SLIPPED AWAY FROM US. WE FEEL SUCH SORROW AND
DEEP SADNESS. YET WE ARE SO THANKFUL FOR YOUR VITAL
SPIRIT. WE HAVE BEEN BLESSED BY KNOWING YOU. YOUR LIFE
TOUCHED US.

WITH DEATH COMES MEMORIES. THOSE MEMORIES REMIND US OF
THE RICHNESS THAT WAS YOU.

YOUR FAMILY. YOU LOVED YOUR FAMILY - AS MAD AS WE ALL
COULD MAKE YOU. OF COURSE YOU HAD YOUR MOMENTS OF MAKING
US PRETTY LIVID TOO. DINNER CONVERSATIONS WERE OFTEN
INTERESTING. THEY COULD PROBABLY BEST BE DESCRIBED AS
MONOLOGUES FOR THE EDIFICATION OF CHILDREN. OUR MOST
EFFECTIVE DEFENSE WAS TO RAISE OUR HANDS TOGETHER IN
SILENT PROTEST WHEN WE HAD HEARD ENOUGH. YOU WERE
GRACIOUS ENOUGH TO GET THE RATHER BLATANT HINT AND
POLITELY TELL US ALL TO GO TO HELL. THEN THERE WERE THE
JOKES. HOW MANY OF YOU AS FATHERS BROUGHT HOME DIRTY
JOKES TO TELL THE KIDS AT THE DINNER TABLE? KATE,
SOMEHOW, NEVER THOUGHT THEY WERE VERY FUNNY!

KATE. YOUR FAMOUS QUOTE SAID AT A LUNCHEON GIVEN IN
HONOR OF BOTH YOUR ACCOMPLISHMENTS AND CONTRIBUTIONS.
"DO YOU HAVE ANY IDEA HOW DIFFICULT IT IS TO LIVE WITH
QUIET POWER FOR 40 YEARS?" YOU AND KATE WERE A TEAM. I
LOVED YOU FOR TELLING ME HOW IMPORTANT MOM'S SUPPORT WAS
IN MANAGING OUR FAMILY AS YOU WORKED TO GROW AND
STRENGTHEN PACIFIC AIR FREIGHT AND THEN AIRBORNE. HOW
CAN WE FORGET YOUR WORDS ON THE ANSWERING MACHINE? "KATE
AND HOLT ARE VERY BUSY RIGHT NOW. PLEASE LEAVE A MESSAGE
AT THE BEEP." FOR ALL YOUR CHAUVINISTIC WAYS YOU TRULY
LOVED, RESPECTED AND SUPPORTED MOM FOR HERSELF, HER
TALENTS, HER CONTRIBUTIONS. YOU INCLUDED HER TOTALLY IN
YOUR LIFE - A WONDERFUL GIFT.

YOUR GRANDCHILDREN. HOW YOU LOVED AND SUPPORTED YOUR
GRANDCHILDREN. BEN EXPRESSED HIS FEELING ABOUT GRANDPA'S
DEATH BY SAYING: "I'M DOING OKAY BUT NOW WE WON'T HAVE
ANYONE TO TELL US JOKES." BEN'S WORDS WERE SO SINCERE.
AND SO TRUE. WE'LL HAVE JOKES, BUT NOT GRANDPA'S.

YOUR HUMOR. YOUR WONDERFUL, WONDERFUL HUMOR AND GIFT OF
DELIVERY. YOURS WAS HUMOR AND RUDENESS COMBINED. AS ONE
FRIEND SO APTLY PUT: "HOLT WAS SO RUDE. YET - HE WAS
RUDE WITHOUT MALICE." REMEMBER HOW YOU LEFT VIA THE BACK
DOOR TO GO TO WORK AT 6:30 IN THE MORNING? YOU TOOK IT
UPON YOURSELF TO WAKE OUR TEENAGE NEIGHBOR, A MERE FEW
FEET AWAY IN THE HOUSE NEXT DOOR. EVERY MORNING YOU
YELLED UP INTO BETHIE'S SECOND FLOOR WINDOW: "YOU AWAKE
YET BETH - IT'S TIME TO GO TO SCHOOL!" CHARMING RUDENESS
WAS DAD'S MAGIC.

DAD'S WORK. PACIFIC AIR FREIGHT. AIRBORNE. IT WAS YOUR LIFE AND OURS. WE GREW WITH IT FROM THE LITTLE OFFICE ON MARION, TO THE COLEMAN BUILDING TO ITS PRESENT SITE AT THE BASE OF QUEEN ANNE. AND YET YOU HAD THE GRACE TO LEAVE THAT LIFE'S WORK, TO BACK AWAY, TO LET OTHERS TAKE OVER. I'M SO SORRY YOU MISSED YOUR FAREWELL BOARD MEETING BUT SO THANKFUL FOR WHAT YOU GAVE TO AND WHAT YOU RECEIVED FROM THE PEOPLE AT AIRBORNE.

YOU WERE A MAN OF THE PEOPLE AND COMMUNITY. YOU DIDN'T CARE FOR FANCY WAYS. YOU DIDN'T CARE FOR STATUS AND SHOW. YOU CARED FOR HARD WORK AND A JOB WELL DONE - UNLESS OF COURSE IT WAS YOUR CARPENTRY AND THEN IT COULD BE ALMOST BUT NOT QUITE A PERFECT JOB. YOU CARED FOR SINCERITY, HONESTY AND GENEROSITY. YOU CARED FOR FAMILY AND COMMUNITY. YOU BELIEVED A PERSON SHOULD GIVE BACK TO COMMUNITY. AND YOU DID - THROUGH YOUR OWN GENEROUS GIVING OF MONEY, TIME AND SUPPORTIVE ADVICE AND COUNSELING.

YOU WERE A MAN OF THE PEOPLE BUT LOVED THE SOLITUDE OF THE LAND. BAINBRIDGE WAS YOUR ESCAPE. THERE YOU HAD AN AFFINITY WITH THE RURAL QUIET AND BEAUTY, WITH YOUR VEGETABLE GARDEN AND WITH YOUR MOWER THAT SERVED AS AS ESCAPE FROM ALL THE HOARDES OF FAMILY THAT DESCENDED UPON YOU IN THE SUMMERS. GEARHEART - YOUR CHILDHOOD HOME ON THE OCEAN. I WILL ALWAYS REMEMBER IT AS YOUR FAVORITE VACATION SPOT AND WILL TREASURE THE TOURS OF YOUR CHILDHOOD NEIGHBORHOOD; THE BEACH HOUSE, FRIENDS HOMES, THE TENNIS COURT, THE WIND SWEPT, FLAT GOLF COURSE. YOU HELD A QUIET BUT VERY SINCERE RESPECT AND LOVE FOR THE NATURAL BEAUTY AND PRECIOUSNESS OF OUR LAND. YOU LEARNED TO RECYCLE, TO COMPOST, TO PUT WATER-SAVING DEVICES ON THE FAUCETS. YOU LAMENTED THE GROWTH OF BUILDINGS IN SEATTLE THAT BLOCKED THE VIEWS OF THE SOUND AND CAST SHADOWS ON THE ALREADY SUN-STARVED STREETS.

SO MANY WONDERFUL QUALITIES: YOUR INCREDIBLE ON-GOING SUPPORT FOR OUR WORK AND FAMILIES EVEN WHEN YOU WEREN'T TOO SURE YOU LIKED WHAT YOU SAW: YOUR SELF-EFFACING HUMOR: YOUR ABILITY TO LAUGH AT YOURSELF: YOUR IRREVERENCE. WE GREW UP COMING TO THE 10:30 SERVICE HERE. WE SAT IN THESE VERY SAME PEWS - IN FACT JUST ABOUT RIGHT OVER THERE. DAD LIKED HIS ROUTINES. DEAN LEFFLER WOULD LEAD THE SERVICE AND AT THE APPROPRIATE TIME HE WOULD ASK US ALL TO SHARE IN A MOMENT OF SILENT PRAYER. AT THE CLOSE HE WOULD CONTINUE ON. DAD WOULD LEAN OVER TO ME AND SAY, "I GOT TO 100 HOW FAR DID YOU GET?" THEN HE'D PULL OUT THE GIFTING ENVELOPE AND THE STUBBY YELLOW PENCIL AND START A GAME OF TIC-TAC-TOE.

HOLT WAS A PERSON TO BE LOVED AND ADMIRED. HE IS A PERSON TO BE MISSED. HOLT GAVE US MANY BLESSINGS THAT I HOPE WE CAN KEEP WITHIN OURSELVES, TO REMEMBER, TO CHERISH AND TO SHARE WITH OTHERS. WE'RE SO PROUD OF YOU DAD. WE'LL MISS YOU. GOD BLESS YOU DAD. GOD BLESS US ALL.

Anne

Remembering Bainbridge Island
HOLT WILSON WEBSTER
1992

I was on the 6:15 ferry last Tuesday, walking the upper deck, thinking of what to say about Dad to you, his family and friends.

The **air** was exceptionally still, as if it were holding its breath between weather systems. The **water** was glassy smooth with an easy roll, broken only by the ferry's wake, a few gulls and a hungry california sea lion in the distance. The **sky** was blue and clear above, but thick steel grey clouds were gathering on each horizon.

Suddenly I imagined a conversation with Dad which began,

> " Lewis, It's Holtie,... Just open your eyes my friend because it's there in front of you".

> "Ask them why **they** are here... and you can offer a few opinions from me if it helps".

> "Here? I asked...You mean, like on earth?". "NO," he said patiently,
> " keep it simple."

> "At Saint Barnabas, today". "Now don't get me started," he answered.

> "**BAINBRIDGE**," I exclaimed, "On Bainbridge." He smiled and nodded yes.

Bainbridge Island, to Dad **was life** as he wanted it to be.

A place to escape from work, to recover and re-group, Free from city hassles.

He loved Bainbridge the community and the friends and family who have made it their home. He was committed to working for the best future possible for the island..

Bainbridge was **SUNNYBRANCH**- always a great place to bring your friends
he always made it a comfortable surrounding for everyone.

It was TENNIS, singles with the kids and doubles with Don, Vern, Mom, Susie and others, under the Nana's critical eye. And of course the traps at Meadowmeer.

It was gardening and chores HOUSEHOLD OPERATIONS to do and complain about humorously at the same time. He had lists checked off we can only aspire to.

It was <u>any</u> evening with his WIFE, his dog and a dry martini.

"Holt!?, Its your Son."

You know Dad, I really think we all do know why we are here, and we will think of you often **because, and despite** your opinions...As we continue

> **Doing** your favorite and not so favorite chores.
> **Playing and watching** your favorite sports.
> **Drinking and Toasting** to your memory.

We will keep on keeping on with those things you enjoyed which make Bainbridge a place to come back to, A place you loved so much. A place you called home.

Holt's Dad & Mother in their Ford, c. 1925

Holt & older sister Mary Ma'Carry, c. 1930

FATHERS AND SONS
HOLT WILSON WEBSTER
1992

Fathers and Sons. It can be a rough road to travel for both. When I was in high school I learned a poem by Robert Frost, about two roads, diverging in a wood. It described a decision to take a less traveled path **in life** and the difference it made.

I think we all knew, Dad followed a very clear, easily identifiable path, **BUT** he never forced anyone, **including me**, to follow it. To be sure, he made executive decisions which became the law, but he backed them up with **trust** rather than punishment. It worked.

A Line in the poem goes,
> "then took the other, just as fair, but having perhaps a better claim, because it was grassy and wanted wear."…

…Well I took other paths, **and I took them often as sons are want to do**. Ask anyone who has had to keep track of my **phone** numbers. Dad would ask a lot of questions, offer a definite opinion and let me go on. He only expected me to be accountable for my actions. It's all he expected of anyone.

He and I had a conversation recently, a phone call that went something like this,

> **"Lewis**, This is **Holt** Webster. I understand you called with a question," he started.

> My list of notes ready to be checked off, I jumped in…,
> Item 1. "Need to raise money Dad, Non-profit
> Item 2. "Maritime Heritage, Education, Kids, Old Ships, good stuff"
>   "HMMPH he responded
> Item 3. "Mayor and City Council are behind the concept,"(credibility)
> Item 4. "Need a bigger support base…etc.etc."

> A short silence. Dad answers, "ok"..Another pause.
> Item 1. "How much"
> Item 2. "who are you asking"
> Item 3. "How are you going to follow up?"
>   and finally, "Well Craig, This is what I'd do."

If you wanted advice or even a response from Holt Webster, **especially if** you were his son, you had better have a plan. He took you at **face value**, and the value went up the better prepared you were. But he also gave you his best, most straightforward answer. Then it was up to you to navigate your own course.

Every son needs the love and approval of his father. As our relationship had changed from **parent to child** into **friend to friend**, Dad's **approval** had come with his enthusiastic support for my new business. His **love and respect** was shown in his own way by the excitment he had about my success. **That was all I could ever ask for.**

It's my feeling that my memories are different from yours only in the context and the intensity. Which ever path we may be travelling on, we each can share in the gifts of honesty, humour, sincerity and trust given to to us by Dad, and use them as as tools for **EVERY** **DAY**,   Holt Webster would be happy about that.
He was an **EVERY** DAY kind of MAN.

The family at home, 1954.

Holt Webster Memorial
St. Mark's Cathedral - April 21, 1992

Ancil H. Payne

I speak not only as a friend of 30 years but, in both age and years of service, the oldest non-management member of the Airborne Board of Directors.

Holt and I met as the result of an annual fund-raising campaign for this, St. Mark's Cathedral. I had been given his yearly pledge card, and called at his home on Newton Street. I don't remember whether it was Ann or Kelly who came to the door and, after racing back to the kitchen, returned to say "Dad wants to know if you can come back a little later; he's cleaning the stove oven." I did, and we became friends. I don't recall just how much Holt pledged, but it was undoubtedly several times greater than his fair share, but appropriately a sum skillfully negotiated down from the original request. Holt was devoted to the church, but he never left his business skills behind the door when he left the office!

He became a chief fund-raiser (and the organ we hear today is one result of his work) and was a confidant of our spiritual adviser, the Reverend John Leffler, for many years the Dean of this Cathedral. He loved this church, so it is most appropriate that we meet here in his memory.

Holt, necessarily, became more closely acquainted with airplanes than he might have wished during World War II when he served as Captain in the Military Air Transport Command and flew the famous Burma Hump in the Himilayas. After the war, he joined Northwest Airlines, where he became more closely acquainted with commercial airline management than he might have wished. His frustration was doubled when it came to Northwest's president, John Nyrop.

Armed with the combined knowledge of the skills -- or mostly lack thereof -- of both military and civilian air transportation management, he moved to a small outfit, Pacific Air Freight, became president, shortly merged his company with California's Airborne Freight, and took over both. From a monumentally muddled operation, with the steady assistance of the two Bobs -- Cline and Brazier -- and the counsel of his lifelong friend, Vern Williams, Holt built a then-struggling freight-forwarding business into an international air-express operation, second or third largest and for eight year the fastest growing air-express operation in the nation: currently a business with over 70 airplanes and a revenue well in excess of a billion dollars. This was not without attention and sacrifice, including personally underwriting company bank loans during periods of financial crisis.

Holt achieved with and through others. His leadership was never complex: he demanded direct, honest discussion from his Board -- and others, loyalty to the firm, and dedication to the job. It did help if you liked martinis!

- 2 -

He was not devious -- and that's an understatement -- and woe be it
to the person who was less than straightforward with him, for he
might better do battle with a D-8 bulldozer. A delicate diplomat
Mr. Webster was not; and a select number of Californians,
Australians, and New Yorkers will so testify. And anyone scratch-
ing at members of his operation, or those he loved or trusted,
might better have picked a fight with a mad mother bear defending
her cubs. His rhetoric in these moments of anger more nearly
approximated that of a swabbie on a Columbia River boat crew (which
at one time he was) than anything offered at Andover Prep. It is
little wonder that Airborne truck drivers, dock workers, and crew
members clearly understood him and devotedly referred to him as
"The Old Man."

On the other hand, Holt never cut, nor was unkind to anyone who was
trying; and, he was interested in the welfare of an Airborne
deliveryman, a community college student, an elderly person
benefiting from his long support of senior services, just as he was
in an officer of his or any other company.

I cannot conclude without observing that, in business affairs, Holt
was solicitous, open-minded and, while opinionated, never
inflexible. In political matters his discipline differed by a few
degrees: about 180! When addressing matters within the body
politic, he fearlessly slayed the political dragons -- particularly
the Democratic Party dragons -- and often disposed of complicated
political problems with stunningly simple solutions. At the
conclusion of some dinner parties where bombastic observations were
rendered, he would pose a seemingly embarrassed nod to Kate and,
with the practiced penance of a 10-year-old, piteously observe that
he guessed he would be sleeping on the couch tonight! In the
matter of politics, Holt may have been wrong, but he was never in
doubt.

It is often said that a company is but the shadow of its president.
The proof of leadership is the legacy the leader leaves. From
almost nothing, and against overwhelming financial and geographic
odds, he built a huge, successful, growing company and he left it
in the hands of Bob Cline, Bob Brazier, and a skilled, experienced,
and well trained management team of real depth, unmatched by any
other organization in the industry. That is a legacy of genuine
value to the community, his shareholders, and to every man or woman
who worked with and for him, for it goes far to guarantee long-term
security.

Someone said the mark of a man's earthly success is whether or not
the world is better off for his having existed. With Holt, it is.

Holt Webster Memorial
Doug Picha

I wasn't sure how to take Holt the first time we met. He was a study in contrasts. He was a little gruff, yet warm and friendly, and had that twinkle in his eye. Yet you could tell immediately he did not suffer foolishness lightly. As Kate would often describe him, "Holt is one of a kind."

I will have four lasting memories of Holt.

The first was his legendary sense of humor and wit. He made you laugh. It was always good to see him, even though you could expect to be quieted with a caustic remark. He didn't take himself too seriously, and as a result, was always fun to be around.

Another memory will be how Holt cared about the people close to him and in our community where he lived and worked. His commitment and contributions were impressive:
* Downtown Rotary where he was a member for 28 years.
* A past president of the Seattle Chamber of Commerce
* Serving on the boards of United Way , Virginia Mason Medical Center, King County Senior Services and Independent Colleges of Washington
* The Vestries here at St. Mark's and at St. Barnabas on Bainbridge Island
* Active with YMCA and Children's Hospital
* And also served as a president of the Seattle Central Community College Foundation. Dr. Charles Mitchell, president of Seattle Central, commented how Holt was a real positive force. Dr. Mitchell was always impressed by his love for the students.

Holt also worked for and advised the small emerging organizations. I was especially familiar with those he helped on Bainbridge Island. If it was creating a private effort to raise funds for our public schools, or building a new performing arts center -- Holt was always there willingly.

His caring for others didn't stop in his capacity at Airborne Freight. When he founded the company, he also created and inspired a corporate culture of giving back. Airborne stands out as a leader today for what it does in the community. In large part this is a testimony to Holt's influence and sense of corporate responsibility.

One of the last conversations I had with Holt a few weeks ago was concerning Children's Hospital's charitable request of Airborne. As only Holt could say, "You want how much? You're kidding, right?"

Bob Cline, the CEO at Airborne and a friend and colleague for 27 years, said
"Holt not only talked about giving back -- but he lived it as well. His example and influence rubbed off on everyone," Bob said. This part of his work was important to him and he took it seriously.

Beyond the impressive contributions he made to the large charitable organizations he served, perhaps his care for others will best be remembered by each of us on a personal level. Holt had that rare ability to accept people as they are. It was easy to be his friend -- because he made it that way.

I asked my wife Cassie what she'll remember most about Holt and without hesitating she said, "He was always so ready to like people."

This feeling was expressed in an eloquent letter written to Holt during his stay in the hospital. It is from a seventeen year old friend of his whom Holt hired to work in his yard. The letter read:

"Dear Mr. Webster,

Having just returned from seeing you this afternoon, I want to express my gratitude for having met you and for the generosity you have displayed in sharing a part of you with me.

Though you may not be aware of it, since meeting you I have gained invaluable guidance and inspiration both from what you have told me and from what I have seen. More importantly, however, you have always displayed to me a sense of confirmation and approval which I have been unable to receive from but a few people. For even during times of my indiscretion and poor judgement, you warmly and openly accepted me. I really have felt no greater honor than to have established a relationship with you, someone I respect so much -- who for no reason other than genuine fellowship, has befriended me.

So I want to openly thank you. Thank you for being a friend and a mentor. I hope that someday I can be as significant a part in other peoples lives as you have been in mine. If I do achieve such a height, I owe a great deal of it to you."

Holt loved being home on his property on Bainbridge Island, especially outside.   I'll never forget one beautiful Saturday in the fall, about eight years ago, when our City Club Board , which kate and I were serving on, was retreating at the Webster house. From the living room where we were sitting, I must have watched Holt ride past the front window 15 times on his lawn tractor pulling a trailer full of wood or compost. Back and forth -- sitting erect -- totally content.

He was so proud of the barn that his son Craig designed and he helped build, which was no ordinary barn. In typical Holt fashion, it was done with and eye to detail and quality.

He would always use choice language to describe how he felt about the crows eating the apples from his trees or the slugs on his strawberries.

When you would ask him how his garden was growing he would tell you his blueberries were getting too much water and more than once he asked me, a fellow gardener, "why do my raspberry plants look like hell?"

Junko Harui (Ha-roo-ee), a friend and owner of the nursery on Bainbridge, said Holt could find a great release with his plants. He loved his garden.

Lastly, I'll forever hold the memory of Holt and Kate -- the couple. They were a devoted and loving team. The YMCA honored them as such in 1984 as the recipients of the A.K. Guy Award for community service. The P.I. headline the following morning read, "Couple Make Volunteering a Way of Life."

Sue Lile, a close friend, said they were each other's best friend. They had a real partnership of support and sharing.

Holt was a good man. He touched and enriched our lives and the lives of others. He celebrated life with gusto, and we're thankful to have known him and his unique charm. Yes, Kate, Holt was 'one of a kind'..... and we'll miss him.

"Craig Webster, passionate Seattle architect, dies in Utah plane crash."
By Christine Clarridge and Susan Gilmore, Seattle Times staff reporters[1]

"Craig Webster died on May 7, 2007, doing one of the things he loved most: flying his Cessna 210. The plane crashed in Utah during an emergency landing en route to Seattle from San Antonio. Craig, a part-time Deer Harbor resident who deeply loved the island, was the architect for OPAL's Bonnie Brae neighborhood [OPAL "Of People And Land" Community Land Trust] and had led OPAL's design process almost to completion on the Mt. Baker Road project before he died. 'Craig had a keen eye for how to make small buildings work', said Lisa Byers. 'His major contributions to the Mt. Baker Road project include a strong aesthetic sense of rural charm in the midst of urban density—based on his fond recollections of his grandparents' farm buildings—and a commitment to green building practices. Craig's special touch remains on the new neighborhood and will be enjoyed and remembered by generations of OPAL home-owners on Mt. Baker Road'." (Summer 2007, OPAL NEWSLETTER, Eastsound, WA, opalclt.org, p. 6.)

Craig Lewis Webster
June 16, 1950–May 7, 2007

---

1   (Thursday, May 10, 2007 - Page updated at 02:27 PM) Source: https://www.seattletimes.com/seattle-news/craig-webster-passionate-seattle-architect-dies-in-utah-plane-crash/

Craig WEBSTER

Craig Lewis Webster celebrated life. He loved people but also thrived on solo adventures where he could directly experience the outdoor elements. His family was extremely important to him. Craig gave all of himself to everything he did whether it was learning a new skill or taking part in the many community projects about which he so cared. Craig's generosity of spirit, his joie de vivre and his quirky sense of humor endeared him to everyone who knew him. He had a passionate, playful and gentle nature, and a unique way of framing the world around him.

Craig's passions included first and foremost his wife, Tasha, and their dog, Sabakka. He was an avid sailor and a talented artist who painted, sketched and photographed with sensitivity and skill. He began each day at 5:00 a.m. regardless of the season, traversing Lake Union in his beloved scull. Flying was his newest adventure. He got his pilot's license to celebrate his 49th birthday! He loved the solitude and beauty of being in the air.

Craig was the founder of the Seattle firm, C.L. Webster Architects. Over his career he designed a wide variety of projects, including affordable housing, medical clinics, community centers, and residences. He approached each project with a fresh enthusiasm and vision, and found beauty in the details as well as the big picture.

Craig's sense of service to his community was a huge part of who he was. He was very interested in designing affordable housing and incorporating sustainable design principles into his work. Recently Craig led a team to Mississippi, providing relief to communities devastated by Hurricane Katrina. Craig served on the boards of the Maritime Heritage Foundation, Northwest Seaport and Architects without Borders.

Craig was a family man. Though he had no children of his own, his three nieces and three nephews were a cherished part of his life and he of theirs. "Uncle Cwaigy" was a great uncle - fun, funny and hip. He offered a shoulder to cry on and strength in times of confusion or pain.

Craig is survived by his wife, Tasha, his mother, Kate Webster, his sisters, Kelly Webster and Anne Fox, his brother-in-law, Jon Fox, his nieces, nephews and grand-nephew. He brightened our lives, and we will miss him terribly.

Craig was returning from an AIA Convention in Texas when his Cessna 210 developed mechanical problems. Craig died when the plane crashed as he attempted an emergency landing.

A Memorial Service for Craig will be held at 2:00 p.m. on Tuesday, May 15, at St. Mark's Episcopal Cathedral, 1245 10th East, in Seattle. Remembrances may be sent to Northwest Seaport.

Copy written by Craig's sisters Kelly and Annie.

"Before the wedding" (October 2004) Rex Bond (best man), Tasha, Kelly, Craig

184

"A sister's Reflections On the Life Of Her Brother" by Annie Webster Fox

This gathering is an honor to Craig's name and memory. Thank you for joining us to remember Craig, to show your support for Tasha and our families, and to grieve in communion with us.

Twelfth & Newton. The house we grew up in. Craig's room was on the third floor. He had a commanding view north, overlooking Portage Bay, the U District, neighborhoods, city streets and city lights beyond. It was a pilot's view from the cockpit, his plywood slab desk installed against the window, allowing him to sit facing the view. His bed squeaked. I could hear it from the second floor. He'd stand at the top of the attic stairs wearing his dress clothes, gray slacks, coat, black shoes and white socks, daring his parents to challenge his fashion sense.

Challenge he did and yelling matches ensued.

War games with neighborhood buddies. Cap, EG, Scott and others. Those were games on the street, in the playfield. Nothing virtual back then. From that neighborhood, Craig formed lifelong friendships that live to today.

Schools. Lakeside, a community that, again, brought Craig links to lifelong friendships. The Seward School, grades K-5. The floating home, such a poetic description Tasha chose for what most call a houseboat, is only two blocks west of the elementary school he attended. He'd walk up to the school playground with his beloved and indulged dog, Sabaka, for daily runs.

Craig came back to Place, this City, his home.

In his writings, Wendell Berry reflects: Make a home. Help to make a community. Be loyal to what you have made. That was Craig.

Bainbridge: More family. More lifelong friendships. Jeff, Carl, The South End Gang. Summers on the water sailing, water-skiing. Family doubles on the tennis court and singles with his younger sister, me. For years I beat Craig by simply staying calm. I let him play against himself.

His anger towards himself made him famous. Why was it there? His expectations were so high, especially in judgment against himself. It was sometimes painful to watch.

He got his payback though. He took me for a sail in a small boat on Lake Michigan one spring when I visited him while he attended grad school in Milwaukee. The water was rough and he was in command, keeling the boat over as dramatically as possible to enjoy the look of terror rising across his sister's face.

Road trips. Craig and I were one year apart in school. We both attended college in the east. He had the car. We'd pick a different route to travel across the country going to school and coming home. Sometimes Karin drove with us. Highway 1 across Canada, Highway 94 across the northern US. Highway 80 across the central US. Highway 40 across the southern US. It was the early 70s and the south wasn't too friendly to longhaired, bearded young men and longhaired, scraggly girls dressed in jeans and lumberjack coats. At one KOA campground we had to convince them we were brother and sister, and that we could safely tent together without forever condemning ourselves to Hell.

Craig loved an adventure. That's how he died isn't it? It's important we remember, however horrifying and sudden the tragedy, that for him to have denied himself an adventure would have had the unthinkable result of shrinking his horizons, of limiting his freedom.

Skiing and hiking in our teens and twenty's. Crystal. Goat Rocks, Wilderness. The Smokey Mountains. The Grand Canyon. The Isle of Skye. We could sport in companionable silence.

Craig lived for the release (again to borrow words from Tasha) that the outdoor elements wind, water, air, gave him. His solos on the ocean. His rowing on The Lake. His flying. His cabin getaway on Orcas.

Design. Craig was the master of design not just architecture but also of sketching, packaging gifts, decorating. He brought his style into every facet of his life and of his giving. He put pen to paper and, in many cases, hammer to nail. His completed work includes homes, communities, even (thankfully only one) a marina. Bathrooms. His bathrooms were fabulous. Cass described him as 'The Cubbyhole Guy. He used compartmentalization to fit a boat, a plane, his architectural style. Our home is a design by Craig. We worked together, Jon and I, the builder Odyssey

Cabin at Spring Point, Orcas Island   CLW

and Craig to design and build a lovely home. It is his gift to us. For me, his living memory.

Family. Craig didn't have children but that didn't mean he didn't value family. He cared deeply for his own family, for Tasha and her family. He treated his friends as family, re-formed his ties to changed relationships to maintain those connections. He was generous, sometimes to a fault. I weep for Mom over the loss of her only son. His companionship to her. The confidences they shared. His careful oversight of the wear and tear, the condition, of Sunnybranch, our Bainbridge home. It is left to Kelly and me, poor substitutes on that score!

Craig packed a lifetime into his 56 years. Keeping busy. Rushing to get the next task done. Those were trademark traits. We'll miss him. We'll both grieve our loss and celebrate the richness he brought to our lives.

I'll close with this haiku from an 18th century Japanese poet, Yosa Buson. They are words by which to remember Craig's affinity to the sensory in design, in the outdoors, in his life:

Misty grasses,
quiet waters,
it's evening.

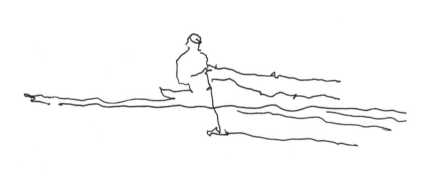

Craig's drawing of his cabin was done in 2005.
He drew the rowing picture around 2006, one year before his death.

Craig's Birthday Surprise June 1999

On Craig's houseboat, Lake Union, for his 49th birthday. In the middle of the party, Craig said, "Sorry, Mom, I forgot something. Back in a few minutes." Typical of Craig's style, a few minutes later, one of his buddies, Rex, said, "Come on out to the dock, Kate."

Dave Rutherford in rowboat

A single-engine plane landed on its pontoons and pulled up to the dock. To my astonishment, Craig was the pilot—he had just gotten his license!

Flying had been a long-time ambition for Craig, but none of us knew that he had been taking lessons all winter to prepare for that day.

Memories Of Craig

Craig was our middle child and only son. That combination set him up for a unique position in our family. Over the years he and I developed an untypical mother-son relationship. It was really his doing. Craig never treated me with any real *reverence*, but rather almost always with a big grin on his face and, I believe, in his soul. As a child he questioned almost every request, usually, like his father, with some hint of humor. What gave me the advantage is that Craig could not lie with a straight face. That saved us both a lot of grief, especially in the early years.

Skiing, sailing, flying—these activities with Craig were always fun and a learning experience. He loved to push me beyond my own comfort level. But his coaxing—and cajoling—usually produced at least some results.

Craig's death has left in me, in my heart, a deep and abiding sadness.

Memories, even those of happy times, can still bring tears.

But the fact is that Craig did all the things he dreamed of. Somehow he managed to squeeze into his life one dream after another, whether his college degree, graduate studies, world travel, sailing his own boats, building his own cabin on Orcas Island, and learning to fly! Maybe it is better to be done in by one's dreams than by one's regrets.

I'm a lucky mom to have had such a loving son, who willingly shared so much of his life with me. Nonetheless, Craig's untimely death will always leave an empty space in my heart.

Craig's last Mother's Day card

Part VII

Travels With Kate

Introduction

For the greatest part of my life, traveling was not high on my agenda. I enjoyed reading about far-away places but did not ever expect to see them. My first recollection of real adventure was when, at nine years old, I watched my mother pack her trunk for her two months trip to Vienna, Austria.

Mom had been offered a fellowship to work with a renowned ear, nose, and throat physician in Vienna. Mother was thrilled. I saw her folding all her fancy evening dresses along with her everyday things, and I wondered if she ever would return to us. Her stories all made it sound like a beautiful dream, which in 1933 Vienna it probably lived up to, and for her it certainly did.

My first real trip was later, when my Nana Belcher took ten of her family on a short spring vacation cruise to Bermuda. Most exciting to me was the captain's dinner the final night, when all the waiters marched into the darkened dining room bearing, shoulder-high, platters of baked Alaska all ablaze with brandy sauce. That dessert has always been a favorite of mine and often a Christmas dessert for the Webster family.

Then, for my seventeenth birthday, in April, Dad took sister Suzie, one of my best school buddies, and me to Nassau. The evening of my birthday was unforgettable. We attended a huge gala buffet dinner at the Royal Victoria Hotel. As the music started, in walked the Duke and Duchess of Windsor, "Edward and Wallis." They waved and greeted us all graciously, and then, as the band kept playing, my father asked me to dance—for the first time ever. Dad was extremely musical but hated to dance. The only other time we "stepped out" together was at my wedding.

The years that followed were the WWII era, college for me, marriage, three children, struggling to help establish Holt's business, being a mom and a professional volunteer. Holt and I had an occasional week or two holiday, but always on the West Coast or in Hawaii.

When the kids were eight, ten, and twelve, Holt decided he should take off for a little family time—to go camping. We drove east of the mountains, the Cascades, to Grand Coulee, Moses Lake, White Fish Montana, then to Yellowstone, where we set up camp.

One night we stayed in a populated campground. Kelly, Annie, and Craig took one tent, while Holt and I slept in the back of the station wagon where we quickly fell fast asleep. Sometime in the night we were awakened by a banging on the back window. "There's a bear scraping at your kids' tent!" came the voice out of the night. We clambered out of the station wagon and tiptoed all in a rush over to their tent. The man informed us that the bear had nosed around then retreated. So, for better or for worse, Holt and I spent the rest of the night in the tent with the kids. We had stowed all our food away correctly, so as not to attract animals.

Next morning we prepared the breakfast fire and cooked pancakes. Finishing cleaning up, Holt placed the large 12" iron skillet, which had been my grandmothers, against a tree to dry. A moment later a big black bear grabbed the pan and set to licking off whatever remaining grease it seemed to have smelled.

"Holt!" I cried, "We can't lose that pan!"

He replied, "The bear will drop it. We can wait."

And the bear did.

Holt never let me forget I'd asked him to wrestle a bear to retrieve a frying pan!

Over the last three decades, international travel has become more creative, more frequent, and, relatively speaking, more affordable. It has been my good fortune to have visited many countries all over the globe and seen natural and manmade wonders that take the breath away. Trips abroad included visiting with people who have virtually nothing of value in our material world but can smile and be optimistic. All of these experiences are humbling and, if I may use today's dialect, "truly awesome." People all over the world are basically friendly and curious and willing to share, if given the opportunity as individuals—not driven or hampered by cultural differences or powerful leaders.

It was in my forty-forth year, 1968, that the opportunity for a trip abroad arose. Kelly was spending her junior year of college in Paris, and we had a delightful two week's road trip around England and Scotland. (I wrote of this trip earlier on in the memoirs, on page 72.)

The year 1968 marked the merger of Pacific Air Freight and Airborne. Holt's new role, CEO of Airborne, kept him completely involved for several years. He traveled throughout the Far East and Europe organizing and over-seeing the company, and I kept busy at home with my volunteer activities.

In the spring of 1975, Mother and Dad called from New York and asked if Holt and I would accompany them to Puerto Rico for a short visit with their friends, the Sterns. Mother and Dad didn't feel comfortable traveling alone at their age, and they thought we would enjoy a few days in that lovely climate along with them.

We arrived and were met by the Sterns. Holt and I were taken to the Dorado Beach Hotel, which, built in 1958, was originally a Laurence Rockefeller estate. Right on the beach, it had cabins for individuals or families, a lovely pool, tennis courts, a golf course, and a casino, all attached to the resort.

Mother and Dad went off to have a good visit with their friends, while Holt and I enjoyed ourselves playing tennis, relaxing, and swimming in gorgeous, blue, warm water.

The day after we arrived, we were on the beach about to go swimming when I heard Mother call, "Come here, come here, I want you to meet somebody." We walked up the beach to where they stood and were introduced to Laurence Rockefeller, who was one of mother's patients in New York City. He was charming and asked us if we were enjoying our stay. We told him it was wonderful and the cabin was just perfect for us. Holt said,

Remembering a happy trip Holt and I took to Puerto Rico with Mother and Dad. We stayed at the Dorado Beach Resort Hotel, swam, and played tennis.

as only Holt could do under the circumstances, "There is one problem." When asked what the problem was, he said, "Everything's fine, except I can't get the shutters to close properly at night. So Mr. Rockefeller said, "Let's go look." In the cabin, after a minute, Mr. Rockefeller said, "Oh, well, I think they just need a good shaking and pulling." Holt said, "But they could break." And Laurence Rockefeller replied, "It's ok, I own the place." He then proceeded to give them a thorough shaking, and they worked. We thanked him, and enjoyed the rest of our stay immensely.

In 1976, Holt announced that he was ready for a real vacation, a whole month. He wanted to spend it all in the UK. We drove from London around Kent, Sussex and Devonshire, up through the Cotswolds, the Lake Country, lowlands and Scottish Highlands. The Isle of Skye, Edinburgh, and back down the east side to London.

We planned and booked our Inns and Manor Houses well ahead. A few weeks before leaving, Annie told us she had a month off between jobs and could she come with us. Of course we told her "Yes!" and booked her trip as well. Then we got a call from Craig, who had taken off a year between college and graduate school and was enjoying his version of a "grand tour." He had seen little of the UK and wanted to join us in Troon, Scotland. "Great! We'll see you there," we told him.

We began with a week in London. Holt did some business, and Annie and I toured in a Rolls Royce with a chauffeur that our friend Ned Skinner had offered us. He and friends used it when they traveled in England. Annie was embarrassed by the opulence of this way of traveling, and she insisted on sitting up front with "Barry." So I enjoyed sprawling in the leather luxury of the rear seat. The hotel doorman was very impressed with our "wheels" and treated us like royalty.

Some days later, at "teatime," a call from the desk announced in a cold voice that there was someone there who said he belonged to our party. His name, the manager announced, was Craig! Our unexpected son had turned up bearded, in lederhosen shorts and sandals, with a pack on his back! He certainly startled the concierge and succeed in leaving his father speechless. After a shower and a beard trim, he was quite presentable in long pants, white shirt and jacket.

We managed to book him into all our stops and the four of us had a marvelous time. Annie and Craig liked to hike and that gave Holt and me the time to relax occasionally. It was a treat to travel with grown-up children, lots of laughs and good cheer.

In the late 1970s and early 1980s, Holt asked me to accompany him as he visited his established offices abroad. We had a great trip to several major centers in Australia, as well as a long weekend exploring the Great Barrier Reef.

Traveling around New Zealand followed: from Auckland to Milford Sound and cities in-between. What a treat it was, and such welcoming greeting in each new city, even those in which we didn't know anybody.

Next an Airborne business trip to Hong Kong and Singapore, Tokyo, Osaka, and Kyoto—as Holt worked, I toured and was spoiled by Airborne personnel.

Except for some business trips with Holt, the big trip we took together was when he retired. Airborne sent us around the world first class. In 1984, as a "goodbye" from the company, Holt and I were given a red-carpet trip to all the foreign offices of Airborne Freight. It was a five-week adventure and we were treated royally at every stop. We saw important parts of each country with native guides who were extraordinarily educated and gracious in sharing their local history and stories.

Kawa'i, 1985

One surprise trip took place in early 1990.

My friend Janet Skadan and I were wondering what to give our husbands, Bud and Holt, for Christmas. Off the top of my head I suggested a trip to Disney World, Florida, for a four-day weekend.

We decided we'd do that for the four of us and set the date for January 25th through February 1st. We had a fun time—without going on one ride—and we also spent a day at Cape Canaveral.

We had a truly great time and lots of laughs.

Life changed dramatically for me after Holt died in 1992, much too early in his retirement, and I was still attempting to develop a whole new life plan when Anne and Bill Bowden—dear friends with whom we had traveled several times over the years invited me to go with them on a wonderful trip to China. The excursion included five days on the Yangtze River (before the dam was built). This unforgettable experience rekindled my appetite for seeing more of the world and inspired me to announce to my children and extended family that I was available to go anywhere.

The years since have been filled with adventures of every kind.

It is a very special treat for a mother to be able to travel with just one grown child at a time, and I have been lucky enough to experience this several times. Tours with grandchildren are also extraordinary, a great learning experience for all and an opportunity to know each one as an individual. My sister, cousins, and friends have also been favorite travel companions over the years.

Describing the continuing series of personal adventures in any detail would take another whole book, and would surely not interest anyone except the writer. But as travel has been a major part of my life of late, it seems appropriate to at least supply an overview of the trips I have taken and with whom I have shared these delightful journeys.

World Traveler—What's Important Is The Shoes You Wear

As I recall those Airborne trips before Holt died, they were fascinating, informative, and fun. The following are highlights of my wanderings around the world, not listed in chronological order but rather in a loose geographical account.

Starting with Stonehenge in 1976, I watched the June sun glinting through that astronomical circle of watch-stones. That was a time when one could wander freely among those ancient stones.

A Smith College and 40th wedding anniversary trip in 1987 included a cruise from Stockholm to Oslo across North Sea to Scottish Highlands, including the three islands of Sky, Iona, and Shetland.

Then came five days in Normandy, reviewing the horrors of D-Day. A retired Army Colonel was our excellent guide. He said, "This is really wonderful for me; now I'm retired I can say anything I want." And indeed he did share some heartwarming stories with us.

In Amsterdam, Holland we went to the Van Gough Museum. We viewed his art treasures, "Wheatfield's Under Thunderclouds," "Wheatfield With Crows," "The Potato Eaters."

Next we came to Norway. I loved the "Viking Ship Museum" in Oslo! And later, sitting on a lawn overlooking a fjord, we listened to a wonderful Grieg concert—an unforgettable experience.

In Stockholm, Sweden we visited the Nobel Peace Center, then took the train from Stockholm, over the mountains to Oslo, stopping for lunch at the summit.

Geographically, the next stop was Finland. We spent four hours in Helsinki on a marvelous tour of the city, visiting some famous examples of buildings by the Gesellius, Lindgren, and Saarinen architectural firm, which was formed in 1896.

St. Petersburg, New Year's Eve, Craig and I were dressed in party clothes. We enjoyed a glorious old fashioned cultural celebration with champagne cocktails, followed by wonderful native dancers on the manor house stage, and a full-course dinner. Afterwards, while dancing with Craig on the balcony, I started to laugh. Craig asked, "What's wrong?" I replied, "Do you recognize the music?" He didn't. It was one of my old favorites, "Smoke Gets In Your Eyes."

One memory which most impressed me was our four days driving the *Romantische Strasse* (Romantic Road), between Stuttgart and Strasburg. We spent one night in the Rothenburg ob der Tauber, visiting the shops in "Christmas Town" and also a Thimble Factory.

Budapest, Hungary, an evening cruise on the Danube, we viewed old castles as we cruised under the city's seven bridges, or Seven Gates, five of which had to be rebuilt after World War II.

On the trip to Germany I took with Tasha, we visited Hitler's "Eagle's Nest" (*Kehlsteinhaus*). This mountaintop fortification was a retreat for Hitler to entertain friends, constructed by Martin Bormann and presented on behalf of the National Socialist Party to Hitler for his 50th birthday. "It was a gorgeous view, but also a scary place to be."

While visiting Vienna, Austria, I attended a fabulous Mozart concert with period instruments and costumes. There was also an open air opera featuring life-sized puppets. These puppets could act out the opera in a much more lively way than would have been possible for live actors!

In 1994 I traveled to Italy with Suzie and Mother, who was 97 years old at the time, and we enjoyed a number of exciting adventures. But for me, a high point of that trip was staying in a beautiful hotel on the Grand Canal in Venice and climbing aboard our private yacht for an excursion to the Venetian island of Murano where they make famous glassware.

In Spain, traveling with Bobbie O'Brien, a longtime Brearley buddy, we were able to visit the new Guggenheim Museum Bilbao shortly after it opened.

The entire city of Dubrovnik still showed signs of the 1991 civil war when we visited it in 2006. Nonetheless, the people were warm, friendly, and hospitable. All along the waterfront were walls with paths atop them. Walking along these walls, the destruction from the Croatian War of Independence was still evident 15 years later.

The last European destination was the volcanic Greek island of Santorini. One may hike the steep climb up from the dock, or take a donkey, or a lift-tram – which is what Sarah and I did. Archeologists have been unearthing the fascinating remains of a prehistoric city, Akrotiri, which we visited.

Cappadocia, Turkey, the ancient cliff dwellings, we climbed on ladder into a dwelling. Inside it felt amazingly comfortable. We also descended into the seven floors of caves where people would live during invasions. There were chimneys which routed cooking smoke far away from these refuges so enemies could not locate their shelters.

Our travels in Turkey also included a two day river excursion into valleys steep with rocky crags filled with ancient burial caves. We spent another two days exploring the famous sprawling public market loaded with every imaginable local wares. My favorite purchases were copper pots of different sizes—I had a box of them shipped home, and I still enjoy each piece. The Turkish seaport of Samson included wonderful archeological relics discovered all along the surrounding seacoast.

Traveling to the Middle East included a trip to Abu Dhabi, the capital and the second most populous city of the United Arab Emirates. In 2006 the city was experiencing amazing growth, with construction everywhere. I recall looking out our hotel room window one morning and counting 34 highrise cranes dotting the skyline. There seemed to be no effort at a coherent city plan, just random skyscrapers rising everywhere, each new building unique in architecture and design. The city itself bustled with life, and everyone seemed to be rushing busily to participate in this new metropolis blossoming in the western Arabian desert.

The Maldives are southwest of Sri Lanka in the Indian Ocean. These exotic islands, averaging six feet above sea level, are now vulnerable to planet-wide climate change and sea level rise. Sally Berke and I had a lovely little cabin with our own ladder right down into the bay. Two of my favorite memories are receiving my first hot stone massage and spending the morning with Sally in a submarine moored along a high cliff. We spent a half hour there watching fish along the starboard side and then another half hour portside. What an amazing view!

Cambodia, Angkor Wat. My vivid memory of this network of over 100 Buddhist Temples was the long high wall as one approached the ancient city, with its myriad carvings and bas reliefs. I recall the hot, breathless climb up to the very top.

India. Our trip to the Taj Mahal on the Yamuna river was simply incredible! We arrived at 8:00 PM at the gate, and walking through it the full moon shone down on the white domed mausoleum which seemed to float in the air as the river fog rose to the top of the hill. The guides were dressed all in black and carried flashlights as the sole illumination once inside. At this time one was still allowed into the crypt to see the actual tombs of Mumtaz Mahal and Shah Jahan in the lower level. Marble screens surrounded the biers with prayers were written on paper and tucked within. (Visitors are no longer allowed in the crypt, and replica marble sarcophagi have been put in the entryway.) The whole experience was very emotional for me. As we left, turning back I had a vision I've kept with me to this day.

Mongolia. Our few days in Mongolia before the Silk Road trip was for me unbelievably moving. We slept in a yurt and everyday rode jeeps through the Gobi Desert. From the lowlands to the higher mountains, we saw many aspects of desert life, herds of camels and sheep, and visited the spot where purportedly the first dinosaur eggs were discovered by Roy Chapman Andrews, on an American Museum of Natural History expedition of 1922–23, and whose findings were published in 1924. An unusual summer rain left the desert blooming green and lush. Annie's desire to ride a Mongolian horse, a small and sturdy bread unchanged since the time of Genghis Khan. Her dream was fulfilled on our last day, and it made the trip complete. The owner found a leather saddle—Mongolian saddles are made primarily of wood—and after proving her ridding skill, she was allowed to take the reins herself and had a wonderful ride.

China. The day we visited Beijing the air was so polluted it was hard to stay outside very long and that made it difficult to visit many of the ancient sites. Walking along the Great Wall, I couldn't believe I was there, one of the oldest places I'd ever been. (One of the things I have learned from all my travels, particularly in China, is the importance of the shoes you wear.)

The Silk Road trip from Beijing to the end of the Great Wall, stopping daily in small towns along the way, I enjoyed learning about the local culture and people.

Tibet. Flying into Tibet was one experience I had never thought possible. At that time, 2006, at the airport there were a few jeeps filled with Chinese soldiers, but no other evidence of Chinese occupation. They seemed to be keeping a low profile. Visiting the monasteries and temples was extraordinary in that they were all beautifully decorated, welcoming, and filled with calm. The entry steps to many of them were very steep, each step quite high, and for me hard to climb, so I had to use a cane.

The Potala Palace in Lhasa was built in the 1600s at an altitude of over 12,000 feet. It took me 45 minutes to climb the great staircase just to reach the palace entrance. And then it took longer to climb the six floors to the top. But the spectacular view made it well worth the ascent.

On our final day in Tibet Annie and I drove out to visit the Samye Monastery in Dranang, Tibet's oldest monastery, founded in the eighth century. While we enjoyed a picnic there, after traveling through a number of villages and seeing many yaks, Annie said to me, "We don't need to see any more temples!"

The trip to Bhutan with Kelly, Annie, and Francie Ringold was planned so we could shift roommates at every move. It helped us happily catch up with one another—a great plan that worked well. The countryside was spectacular, mountains and streams and the green landscapes of rice fields abounded. Bhutan is a very fertile country, whose motto seems to be "everyone should be happy!" The atmosphere is everywhere warm and friendly. On the other hand the roads are narrow and two-laned and seem to have no large trucks or busses. We arrived in the capital Thimphu on their national holiday, attended a great celebration in the city stadium with traditional dancing and costumes. Everyone seemed to be there with their whole families, and the warmth and openness was extraordinary. A highlight was a visit to a farmhouse where we were welcomed as old friends, offered tea, and shown the whole house. I was left with a most peaceful feeling of belonging.

Africa. Most impressive to me was in South Africa's Cape Of Good Hope Nature Preserve, where the cold waters of the Atlantic Ocean and the warmer waters of the Indian Ocean meet.

Though Mali and Timbuktu were also wonderful places to visit. And seeing the King Tut exhibit in Cairo at its original home location was likewise unforgettable, as were the giants statues of Luxor. One day in the Serengeti Kelly and I caught glimpses of every type of African wildlife inhabiting the region. And a canoe trip in the shallows in the afternoon afforded views filled with hippos and alligators and paths in the grass along the shore where elephants walked. (A few weeks later, we learned after the trip, that a man was eaten by a lion, right near were we were canoeing!)

In Madagascar we got to see those amazing lemurs. They were so unafraid and playful, they jumped on our shoulders. We traveled there for three luxurious days of crystal clear blue ocean and perfect 80 degrees weather.

My first trip to South America was in 1991 with Holt and the Doctors. We spent a week traveling in a long boat from camp to camp. One day we were crossing some creeks on big fallen logs, which were quite slippery! On one log, I slipped to my knees and lost my glasses into a bunch of seaweed. A fellow traveler kindly was able to retrieve them for me, though I think he was a little put out, saying "Next time I'll find another spot in the line." That was one of the scarier experiences in all my travels.

Another South American trip was to the Atacama Desert, Chile, a stretch of plateau along the Pacific coast, west of the Andes mountains. It is the driest non-polar desert in the world, parts of which have never known rainfall.

Easter Island, with its giant moai statues, and their amazing restoration and preservation. The local inhabitants were so friendly and proud of their land—a wonderful place to visit!

The Iguacu Falls were the most spectacular I had ever seen. They go on for miles, and we had great fun speeding beneath them and getting soaked!

Buenos Aires, Argentina, was a fascinating and elegant city to visit. Old estates and gardens with great trees over 200 years old. We had lunch on one of these estates enjoying native dancers and music.

Finally, closing this summation of my world travels, a trip to Alaska in 2000 afforded me the opportunity to be a part of an adventure tracing the route of the famous 1899 Harriman Alaska Expedition, which included naturalist John Muir and 26 other scientists. Our trip was to be on the 100th anniversary, in 1999, but due to issues with the ship we were delayed one year, and in 2000 we set off aboard the small, 338 feet long, highly maneuverable Clipper Odyssey which accommodated 120 passages and carried 12 Zodiac small boats.

At Ketchikan the original scientific expedition, as was common at the time, had gathered up local artifacts, including Tlingit totem poles and other Inuit relics. Retracing their steps a hundred years later, we brought back to the local tribes two totem poles, native costumes, and some other relics. Tribal leaders were notified ahead of time, and they met us at the Ketchikan docks.

We had a board of professionals from many scientific disciplines lecturing on local flora and fauna, and we took Zodiacs from the ship every day to explore.

The trip started out from Seattle, sailing to Prince Rupert for two weeks. Annie was with me for those first two weeks of the journey. The second two weeks to Nome, Alaska were with Ann Holt.

When in Nome we had a picnic with some of the Inupiat native dancers in costume. Ann, knowing I loved their headdresses bought me one. A month or two later, at the Sunset Club Hat Show, I wore my Alaska native head dress.

Alphabetical List Of Kate Webster's Travels

Country/Location	Dates	Notes
Alaska	2001	1899 Harriman Expedition
American Samoa, **Apia**	2000	Millennium Expedition w/ Kelly
Amazon	1991	w/ the Doctors & Holt
Argentina	2008	w/ Suzie (Patagonia, Atacama Desert)
Australia	1984	Red Carpet Airborne Trip
Austria		
Azerbaijan	2006	w/ Sally Behnke (Dubrovnik)
Botswana	2005	w/ Johnny
Brazil	2004, 2008	w/ Suzie (2008) (Iguacu Falls) Buenos Aires
Bhutan	2010	w/ Kelly, Annie, Francie (Sikkim Unveiled)
Cambodia, Phenom Penh	2000	Millennium Expedition w/ Kelly (& Angkor Wat)
Canada (BC, Yukon)	2001	1899 Harriman Expedition
Chile		
China	1993, 2006	w/ Bowdens (1993), Silk Road w/ Annie (2006)
Croatia	2006	w/ Sally Behnke (Dubrovnik)
Easter Island, **Papeete**	2000	Millennium Expedition w/ Kelly
Ecuador	2008	w/ Suzie
Egypt (Luxor)	2005	w/ Johnny
England (UK)	1976, 1984, 2002	w/ Katherine Fox (2002)
Erie Canal	1998	w/ Bowdens
Finland		
France (Normandy w/Johnny)	1984, 1996, 2008	Red Carpet, Airborne (1984), Normandy (2008)
Galapagos	1998	w/ family
Germany	1984	Red Carpet Airborne Trip
Greece	1995	w/ Sarah Holt Hopper
Hungary (Budapest)	2007	w/ Tasha (inclu. Orient Express)

India (New Delhi, Darjeeling)	2010	w/ Kelly, Annie, Francie
Ireland	1988, 1997	Smith & Holt (in 1988)
Italy	1994, 2007	w/Mom, Suzie (Siena, Florence, Venice), w/Tasha
Japan	1984	Red Carpet Airborne Trip
Jordan	2000, 2006	Millennium Expedition w/ Kelly, w/ Sally Behnke
Kenya		
Korea	2007	
Libya (Tripoli)	2006	w/ Sally Behnke
Madagascar	2005	w/ Johnny
Madeira Island	2005	w/ Johnny
Mali ((Bamako, Timbuktu)	2000, 2005	Millennium Expedition w/ Kelly, w/Johnny (2005)
Maldives Island	2006	w/ Sally Behnke (Dubrovnik)
Mexico		
Mongolia	2006	Silk Road w/ Annie
Montenegro	2005	w/ Johnny
Morocco	2000, 2005	Millennium Expedition w/ Kelly (Marrakech)
Namibia	2005	w/ Johnny
Nepal, Katmandu	2000	Millennium Expedition w/ Kelly
Netherlands		
New Zealand	1984	Red Carpet Airborne Trip
Norway	1988	Smith & Holt
Oman, Muscat	2000	Millennium Expedition w/ Kelly
Papua New Guinea	2000	Millennium Expedition w/ Kelly
Peru	2008	w/ Suzie (Cusco, Manchu Picchu)
Rogue River	1999	rafting w/ Ben & Peter
Russia	1997-98	w/ Craig
Scotland	1988, 2002	Smith & Holt (1988), w/ Katherine Fox (2002)
Singapore	1984	Red Carpet Airborne Trip
South Africa	2005	w/ Johnny

Spain	2004	
Sweden	1988	
Switzerland	1995	
Tanzania, Serengeti	2000, 2005	Millennium Expedition w/ Kelly (& Kilimanjaro)
Tunisia	2005	w/ Johnny
Turkey	1996, 2006	w/ Smith (Anatolia to Ephesus), w/ Sally Behnke
Thailand	1984, 2010	Red Carpet Airborne Trip, w/ Kelly Annie Francie
Tibet	2006	Silk Road w/ Annie
Ukraine (Odessa)	2006	w/ Sally Behnke (Dubrovnik)
UAE (Dubai)	2006	w/ Sally Behnke (Dubrovnik)
Uruguay		
Venezuela		
Wales	1988	
Zambia	2005	w/ Johnny
Zimbabwe		

COLOR CODE: **Europe** / Middle East / Asia / Africa / **No. America** / So. America

Reflections On World Travel

Fascinating, interesting, educational—all the countries I've been blessed to have visited. I've listed and highlighted those key memories of places I recall with special fondness. And in thinking about the travels I've enjoyed—much of spiritual significance and philosophically telling—it can be hard to focus on just the highlights.

One of the things that is different about me, from many people, I've never had a life plan. I've lived my life almost impulsively. When graduated from college, I decided I needed to leave the east coast and be on my own. Went to San Francisco, then Seattle. I had to decide what to do. Things just turned up. And they were wonderful. Holt said, I was just damned lucky to be at the right place right time, especially the growing number of opportunities for women in business and the public arena.

Back in 1946, the reception after Candy's and Chil's wedding was a big party at the McKee's. I discovered that my sister Suzie and I were going out with the same man after the party. He was closer to Suzie's age than mine, so I decided to disappear, pretending a headache. I was heading upstairs to bed when the front door opened, and Holt Webster walked in. Impulsively, I ran over to him and said, "I've been looking for you." And that's how it began, with a conversation that lasted until 3:00 AM. Later he told me he'd come back that night to propose to the widow of an old friend. She didn't accept, Holt came back to party, "And there was Kate." (This might have been a rebound?)

An example of my typically impulsive life, I had just finished as president of the Junior League (in 1962, at the time of the Seattle World's Fair). I had no other plans, and was in bed with pneumonia. The board of Children's Hospital invited me to join them. The board at the time was composed of old Seattle families, it seems to have always been that way. Next, a Smith College opportunity came out of the blue. When Holt died in April 1992 I was out of all my voluntary activities, we had been traveling at that time. This huge change in my life . . . it was then I was invited to become chairman elect of the Smith Board Of Trustees: the main reason was that the college was starting to look for a new president and none of the board members had search-committee experience. They knew I'd been on 7–8 search committees. That assignment lead to the election of President Simmons.

The final involvement that I've had since then is Grace Church on Bainbridge. This time in my life, the development of a new church on Bainbridge Island, and getting to know a whole crowd of island folks who cared about the same spiritual things that meant a lot to me. I'm just so lucky.

The last twenty years have been filled with the incredible number of wonderful trips all over the world which I have here recounted. Traveling with children, grandchildren, cousins and friends has been a privilege and a delight. Each trip has opened my eyes to both the wonders and the tragedies of our world. The physical impact of forests, mountains, glaciers, lakes and deserts has been amazing. The intriguing honesty of local architecture, large and small, in each new area is astounding. The incredible natural beauty of animals viewed in their own territory is inspiring. And the surprising warmth and curiosity and openness with which native people welcome those who show a real interest in them and their lives is heart-warming. "My cup runneth over" with remarkable memories and gratitude for all those who have enriched my life along the way.

Every trip and each fellow traveler has added to my appreciation of our world and the still untapped potential of its inhabitants.

One final vignette was certainly an unforgettable experience for two people who had lived through World War II.

At the end of the Airborne Retirement Trip to the Far East, Holt and I were visiting a monastery in Kyoto. After viewing the gardens, the abbot asked us to follow him to a special area. We entered a long rectangular hall to find about a dozen monks seated on pillows around a beautiful oriental carpet sipping green tea. We were seated with the rest, handed our teacups, and the abbot said that he wanted to tell us about an important event that had taken place in that very space the summer of 1945. Holt and I looked at one another with some apprehension, both thinking of how the war ended in August of 1945 with the surrender of Japan.

This was the room, we were told, where the leaders of Japan—all but the emperor—met to decide how to admit defeat. Their discussion centered around the question of what would or should happen to the emperor. His choices were: to commit *seppuku* (*hara-kiri*), to become a monk and enter a monastery, or to surrender to General Douglas McArthur. The abbot said simply, "The emperor surrendered."

In the ensuing silence I felt emotionally drained and slightly fearful. When I looked up, the monks were all smiling. They raised their cups to us and said together, "Friends."

Holt and I smiled back and echoed: "Yes. Friends."

It was a day and an experience I will never forget.

These Last Two Years

Bringing this story to a close, I entered my 10th decade with a glorious evening on Lake Washington, a celebration with over a hundred family and friends from both Seattle and Bainbridge Island, including my newest great grandchild, MaryKate, just three months old.

2015, I was fortunate to continue my volunteer activities, if at a bit slower pace. Until about a week after my 91st birthday, a heart attack began a year of struggle.

Ted Avery, this last year, has been a Godsend. Starting with the day Ted found me unconscious, through the following months of R&R, he has been a remarkable supporter and my new best friend.

Thanks to both my daughters' steady care and loving attention, I've been thoroughly spoiled.

In May 2016, just after turning 92, I was delighted to attend my 70th Smith College reunion. The requirement for the 70th is that everyone attending needs to bring a "keeper." 23 of us gathered in North Hampton. We all had a great time together.

As I regain my mobility, it was good to feel as though I'd reentered life. Then on June 22nd I enjoyed and was honored at the dedication of the Kate B. Webster Medical Pavilion.

P.S.

Any reader who has gotten this far may have wondered why there has been no reference to the technology explosion of the last 30 years. When Holt retired in 1984, he declared that he had left all technology at Airborne, that he wanted no sign of it at Sunnybranch.

And so it was.

Three months after Holt died in 1992, the president of Seafirst Board of Directors called and told me I was the only board member they couldn't reach in a hurry. He informed me I should be home the following Monday when a FAX machine would arrive.

And so began my introduction to home technology. The next year I bought my first computer, a Hewlett-Packard PC. Over the years I've graduated to flat screen HDMI LED monitors, color laser printers, and Amazon's Alexa personal digital assistant in a small black voice-controlled tube called Echo. And I've come to feel quite at home in the 21st century computer age.

Reflections On Home—Sunnybranch

The seasons change at Sunnybranch with a certain unpredictability, but always the view of our small bay is peaceful. Looking out across the green lawn to the quiet water, where levels rise and fall with the tides and seasons, the surrounding ring of tall stately Douglas firs cast a feeling of strength and stability and serenity down to those of us who live amongst them.

On a foggy, fall morning often even the lawn is hidden from view. Gradually the mist recedes and our sculptured "Blue Heron" appears ready to take flight. Slowly the bay, and finally the trees, can be seen. It is as though the world, our little place in the world, is waking up and waiting to be explored.

Winter on West Port Madison Bay is long and gray and dark and dismal—and peaceful. But occasionally there is a glorious, clear and sunny week to remind us of possibilities ahead; occasionally there are a few days of snow, when the land takes on a new kind of beauty and freshness. And there are memories of afternoons spent reading quietly by a crackling fire. Spring is the glorious season for us with promise of more to follow. Crocuses, daffodils, and tulips begin the brilliant parade, followed by camellias, rhododendrons, azaleas, and countless other shrubs and flowering trees. It is truly a breathtaking sight and one that makes the past dreary months of winter fade away.

As summer arrives our bay fills with boats, resting here briefly on their way north to the San Juan Islands and Desolation Sound. Daily we observe small boats, skippered by neighboring youngsters learning how to sail—a steady and delightful diversion.

Four generations of family gather often on our patio to sun and swim or to read and visit. The kitchen close by is stocked to cover every eventuality.

All this wonder is, for me, truly a glimpse of Paradise at any time of the year. Whether filled with family and friends, or just enjoying in solitude the natural beauty of the land, Sunnybranch is a blessed place.

Heron In Fog, Sunnybranch, Bainbridge Island, sculpture by Elliot Offner.

From time to time I've tried to write
        some words that didn't sound too trite.
Of thoughts and plans and dreams, the kind
        of things that hide down deep in every mind
                and simmer there.
Then as I cast my eyes outside
        and see the gray and gathering mist,
I think that well beyond my sight
        lie answers that I'll never know –
                but they exist.
So maybe if I just relax,
        and stop attempts to sway the facts as life unfolds,
                the words will fly from deep inside,
And so I'll try
        and see what comes.

                                —KBW

Heron In Snow, Sunnybranch, Bainbridge Island, sculpture by Elliot Offner.

Sunnybranch in summer.

Sunnybranch in fall.

Sunnybranch in winter.

Sunnybranch in snow.

Addendum

Drawing of an aerial view of Sunnybranch located in West Port Madison on Bainbridge Island, Washington, drawn by artist Peter Webster

Kate's Dogs

Kate and Fox Terrier Dinty Moore on the beach at Mantoloking, NJ

Toby and Kris

Kris

Heidi

Heidi

Kate and Murmur

Kate and Doobie

Craig and Kelly's Dog Gomer in Green River 1974

Peter and Heidi II

Kai and Lucy

Kai in Summer

Kai in the bushes

Kai in Snow

Zach sleeping

Zach hoping

Walter (Zach's brother) and Nicolas

Chase, Walter, and Nicolas

Kate Belcher Webster,
Accomplishments

Community

2003-2009 - Bush School Board

2000-2007 - Bishop Foundation Trustee: Award Committee

1996-2002 - Executive Service Corps of Washington Board of Governors

1997-2010 - Museum of Flight Board

2000-2001 - Sunset Club Board of Trustees, President (2001-2002)

1981-1987 - City Club Board of Governors (one of eight founders)

1976-1981 - YMCA of Greater Seattle: Chairman of Volunteer Committee; Long-range Planning Committees; Vice Chairman of the Board; Search Committee for Chief Executive Officer

1975-1983 - Seattle Foundation: Search Committee for Chief Executive Officer (Chairman 1980); Chairman of the Board (1981-1983)

1975-1981 - Bloedel Foundation

1968-1972 - United Way of King County Executive Committee

1958-1964 - Seattle Day Nursery Board, Vice President of Executive Committee (1962-1964)

1956-1960 - Council of Aging Board

1958-1962 - Junior League of Seattle Board: Placement Chairman (1958-1960); President (1960-1962)

1947-1956 - Smith Club of Seattle Board: Project Chairman (1956); President (1950)

Corporate

1976-1994 - Seattle First National Bank Board: Organization, Trust, Audit (Chairman 1982-1984), and Public Policy Committees

Education

2012-2016 - Co-president, Smith College, Class of 1946

1983-1995 - University of Washington Business School Advisory Board

1975-1994 - Washington State University Board of Regents: President (1979-1980; 1986-1987); President Search Committee (1984-1985)

1970-1977 - Lakeside School Board

1966-1970 - Saint Nicholas School Board

1946-1950 - Smith Alumnae Fund Class Agent

1981-1986 - Smith Alumnae Nominating Chair for '46

1985-1990 - Smith Alumnae Trustee

1993-1998 - Smith Trustee: Chair Elect (1993-1994); Board Chair (1994-1998)

1999-2004 - Smith College Medal Committee, Chair

Healthcare

1980-1982 - Representative of University of Washington Medical School to American Association of Medical Colleges

1976-1982 - National Association of Children's Hospitals and Related Institutions (NACHRI) Board

1972-1974 - Northwest Kidney Foundation Board

1963-1994 - Children's Hospital and Medical Center Board: Chairman (1970 - 1975)

RELIGIOUS INSTITUTIONS

1998-2004 - Grace Episcopal Church: Chair of Building Committee

1985 & 1989 - Saint Barnabas Episcopal Church Search Committee

1969-1972 - Saint Mark's Episcopal Cathedral Vestry: Search Committee for Dean

Awards

2013 - Outstanding Bainbridge Philanthropist

2004 - Smith College: John M. Greene Award

2000 - Children's Hospital and Medical Center: W.J. Pennington Award

1994 - Washington State University: Kate B. Webster Physical Sciences Building re-named and presented

1993 - Junior League of Seattle: Dorothy Stimson Bullitt Service Award

1989 - Brearley School: Frances Riker Davis Alumnae Award

1985 - AK Guy: YMCA Service Award (with husband Holt Webster)

1982 - Smith College Medal

1981 - University Rotary Club in Seattle: The Paul Harris Award (recognition for distinguished volunteer service)

1977 - Matrix Award: Women in Communications Annual Matrix Award

1977 - Argus Journal (Seattle) Recognition Award

1976 - KIXI Radio, Citizen of the Day

References & Sources

Institutes & Organizations

Falaise, Sand Point Preserve – http://www.sandspointpreserve.org/htm/falaise.htm

Junior League Of Seattle – http://www.jrleagueseattle.org/

Harborview Medical Center – http://uwmedicine.washington.edu/Pages/default.aspx

Washington State Council On Aging – http://www.agingwashington.org/state_council.htm

Seattle Art Museum – http://www.seattleartmuseum.org/

Seattle Gilbert & Sullivan Society – http://www.pattersong.org/

Seattle Day Nursery (now Childhaven) – http://www.childhaven.org/

Seattle Children's Home – http://seattlechildrenshome.org/

Seattle Children's Hospital – http://www.seattlechildrens.org/

City Club – http://www.seattlecityclub.org/

Schools & Colleges

Brearley School – http://www.brearley.org/

Smith College – http://www.smith.edu/

Washington State University – https://wsu.edu/

The Island School – http://www.theislandschool.org/

Sources

Heron Sculpture, Sunnybranch, Bainbridge Island, by Elliot Offner, 1931-2010, Smith College professor of art (http://www.elliotoffner.com/)

Acknowledgements

In my case, "thank yous."

Over two decades ago David Kragen came into my life as I struggled along with my first computer. For these many years I've called him my technology guru, and I've counted on his help whenever I had a computer problem.

The idea of this book originated from Kelly and Annie, who felt I should tell the story for the coming generations. I've taken far too long to complete the job. But, with Dave's gentle prodding, it'll be done as I'm turning 93.

Also, I would like to say "thank you" to my daughters Kelly and Annie, my little sister Suzie, my grandson Peter Webster, and Katherine Johns—all for their encouragement and assistance throughout the process.

To my two remaining cousins, John Ashmun and Russ Belcher, with whom I shared summers through our growing up years, thank you for your occasional assistance in helping me recall some of our escapades—particularly concerning the Far Hills stories.

To Nick Felkey, of Nick Felkey Photo Services, your kind support with image restoration and scanning has been of the highest quality.

To my personal (non-digital) assistant Ted Avery, thank you for your day-to-day encouragement.

Last but not least, to Carol White, you've been a kind and invaluable assistant, neighbor, and friend.

Note from Dave Kragen (2018): Special appreciation goes to Trudy Catterfeld, Island Trudy Consulting, for coming on board the project and meeting with Kate that last year of her life on Earth to guide us through the publication process. The beautiful book you hold in your hands owes its artful form thanks to Trudy's publishing guidance and magic.